EYES **WIDE** OPEN
Going Behind the Environmental Headlines

Paul Fleischman

CANDLEWICK PRESS

Contents

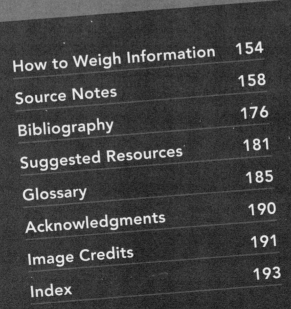

Noticing

optical
illusions

Seeing
what's
really
going on

E verybody lives inside his or her own movie. Mine had usually seemed a light comedy. Then I noticed the first dead bee on the driveway. Then three or four every week. Then the weeks became months. The soundtrack turned ominous. What was this — Stephen King?

When I was a kid, we used to cut out articles about strange goings-on and bring them proudly to school. These were "current events." Interesting fact: they only happened to other people.

The same with history. Every June we turned in our history text-books even though our teachers might only have reached the Model T Ford. Who won World War I? Have a nice summer! History was the dusty past, unconnected to us.

Staring at the bees, I knew otherwise. History is happening right here and right now, whether you live in New York City or, like me, in little Aromas, California, a town too small to merit a traffic light.

What was up with the bees? I wondered. And the environment in

Santa Cruz (CA) Sentinel, 7-13-12

Gas land? Community roused as seismic study seeks oil near Aromas

general. What obstacles are we facing? What solutions have we come up with?

The great thing about history happening right now is that it's all around you. That's also the not-so-great thing. There are plenty of facts, but we're so close to them that it's hard to know what they mean or which ones are important.

The **planning fallacy,** *for example, which causes us to underestimate how long it will take to do something.* Or **normalcy bias,** *the tendency not to take seriously a disaster that's never happened to us before. I fell into the first in writing this book about the second.*

This is especially true today. Adolescence is dramatic and untidy; so are periods when societies change. In times like these, the street-level scene can feel too confusing to comprehend. But in the course of trying to answer those questions, I found some ways to get altitude. Each of the chapters after this introductory section offers a different lens to peer through. Suddenly, we can make out patterns and principles that are driving the headlines. Having names for them will grant you power. You'll begin noticing the same things going on elsewhere — in advertising, politics, and the whole culture we're part of.

It all starts with seeing, and seeing through the everyday world's two biggest illusions.

It's always been this way.

Air-conditioning. Phone calls bouncing off satellites. Clothes dryers and gas lawn mowers. Driving to school and flying cross-country. They're all so common that we hardly notice them, but they're barely older than your baby brother. Over the past two hundred years we found out what coal, then oil, then natural gas, then the atom could do for us, making leaps in agriculture, medicine, and a hundred other fields that have given us the world of wonders we inhabit. No humans have ever lived as we do.

Everything's fine. Technology's

successes have been flat-out dazzling. Now, in our era, its side effects are emerging — the jaws behind the environmental crunch. Modern farming gives us astounding harvests, but its pesticides killed many of the insects that used to pollinate our crops and most likely did in the bees I found. The amazing new world we've created has created new residues. These have led to big unintended problems, from ozone holes to changing climate. These problems were so long-term that we couldn't see them for the first two hundred years. Suddenly, they're in sight, close enough to touch.

This environmental news may turn out to eclipse all the wars and other doings in your history textbooks. Other books and resources will give you much more detail on the science involved. My subject is how we're responding to the writing on the wall, with a focus on the United States. Progress, we now

We can't imagine life without plastic, but it's new on the scene. When the *Titanic* sank in 1912, its passengers' suitcases were leather, their combs ivory, and their toothbrushes made with bone handles and animal bristles.

For a look at some of the everyday chemicals in use all around us and the fight to regulate them, see journalist Bill Moyers's documentary Trade Secrets *at billmoyers.com.*

know, doesn't bring only good things. Causes and effects can be separated by decades and jump over continents. National borders are increasingly beside the point, while the oceans and atmosphere are more important than ever. We're all trying to catch up with these facts. It's a changed world.

I'm no trained scientist. But life is always asking us to get a grip on realms outside our comfort zone, from understanding people different from us to making car-repair decisions. We collect information and chart a course that seems reasonable. "Suggested Resources," on page 181, offers some recommended information sources. Many more

We All Live Downstream

are sprinkled throughout; the book is a door leading to many other doors. "How to Weigh Information," on page 154, gives pointers on judging what you encounter. This is a breaking story, with new data, events, and interpretations arriving daily. For fresh updates as well as info on class-rooms that are reporting on their local environmental scenes, see the book's website, EyesWideOpenUpdates.com.

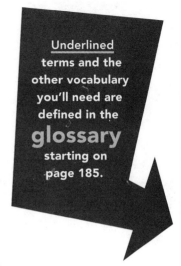

Underlined terms and the other vocabulary you'll need are defined in the **glossary** starting on page 185.

The more I researched, the more I realized that science is only part of the environmental story. Money turns out to be as important as molecules. Science explains what nature is doing; money often explains what *we're* doing. Power and politics are bound up with money. That's why they're included here and why I've drawn on history, psychology, and sociology to help explain what's going on.

What you won't find here: a list of Fifty Simple Things You Can Do to Save the Earth. Instead, the book is a briefing that will launch you on your own list. Notice. Gather information. Reflect. Refine. Act.

You've got power in those acts — what you buy, what you eat, how you get around, what candidates you support, where you throw your energies. The book's goal is to give you a foundation under your decisions.

Let's get started with a quick overview.

Where things stand on five key fronts

the essentials

1 Population

We've just crossed a new threshold: seven billion and counting. If you yawned, the Always-Been-This-Way illusion has you in its grasp. Check out this graph to free yourself:

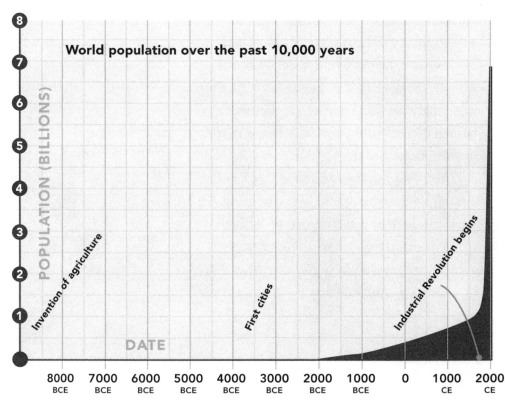

World population over the past 10,000 years

POPULATION (BILLIONS)

Invention of agriculture

First cities

Industrial Revolution begins

DATE

| 8000 BCE | 7000 BCE | 6000 BCE | 5000 BCE | 4000 BCE | 3000 BCE | 2000 BCE | 1000 BCE | 0 | 1000 CE | 2000 CE |

Two restraints kept our numbers low for millennia — food shortage and disease. The spread of New World crops like corn and potatoes, the unlocking of genetics, and improved transportation all helped keep us better fed. Edward Jenner's 1796 inoculation against smallpox was the first giant step in controlling disease, leading to the vaccines you received when you were young and the antibiotics at your pharmacy. When death rates plummeted, numbers shot up. The chains holding population down were cast off.

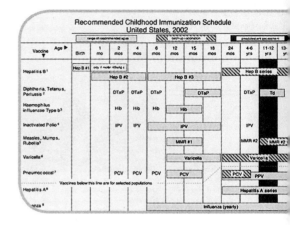

This huge population is flowing out of the countryside and into cities worldwide in search of opportunity. The year 2008 saw more people living in cities than in the country for the first time in history. For many reasons, urban families have fewer children, causing growth rates to fall in the urban **West** decades ago. The same is happening now in most **developing countries,** where four-fifths of the world lives. The highest growth remains in the poorest nations, where birth control is least available and where parents often rely on children for labor but can't assume their young will survive childhood.

Despite falling birth rates, momentum is expected to keep our numbers rising into the next century. Population-tracking

The West:
The most affluent nations, including the United States, Canada, Japan, Australia, and the countries of western Europe.

Developing countries, *sometimes called the* **Third World:** *Predominantly rural nations. Countries in between — China, India, Brazil, and others — are sometimes called* **newly industrialized countries.**

The British economist Thomas Malthus (1766–1834) believed food increases couldn't keep up with population growth, condemning humans to periodic famine.

demographers expect us to add another two to four billion before world population levels off. High-tech advances have let us care for most of our increase to date but their side effects are piling up. It's unclear whether Thomas Malthus will be proven right or wrong. What's certain is that providing that many people with the necessities and luxuries of life from finite resources ties population to every other environmental issue.

2 Consumption

A hunter-gatherer's needs are few, but a Western citizen expects a car, paved streets, hot water on demand, airports, sewer lines, phone service, a refrigerator, computer, microwave, and a PlayStation . . . as a start.

To grasp the import of the Western lifestyle's spread, see the chapter "Our Carbon Copies" in Thomas Friedman's book Hot, Flat, and Crowded. For a close-up look at Western consumption, check out National Geographic's documentary Human Footprint.

To judge impact, population needs to be multiplied by consumption. The items above don't come from the store but from the Earth — from ores and fuels and trees and water. The West holds 20 percent of the world's people but uses 75 percent of its resources to fund its standard of living. From fast food to private cars, that resource-hungry and energy-intensive lifestyle is being adopted by the rest of the world. Soaring population × soaring consumption = unsustainable impact.

Why isn't it sustainable? Scarcity and side effects. The first applies especially to forests, soil, oceans, and freshwater aquifers underground. These resources are renewable, but they're being used up or polluted faster than nature can replenish them. With metals, fuels, and the manufacturing they support, side effects are the bigger issue, from health problems to rising temperatures caused by carbon dioxide (CO_2) and other heat-trapping greenhouse gases.

Unlike Malthusians, **Cornucopians** *(from the Latin word meaning "horn of plenty") dispute claims of scarcity and believe human ingenuity will always keep supplies of food and resources ahead of population. You can read a profile of their best-known spokesman, Julian Simon, in* Wired *magazine's 1997 article "The Doomslayer."*

Even critics of overconsumption, like Reverend Billy and his Church of Stop Shopping, depend on the basic Western lifestyle. Freegans go further than most, walking or biking to get around, bartering and scrounging for used goods instead of buying new ones.

A dead seabird, its stomach cavity filled with plastic trash

After we consume, we toss. Trash and toxins don't stay put. Heavy metals from computers enter groundwater. Tiny particles of plastic are herded across the Pacific by currents. China's air pollution blows east and triggers asthma in California. Sinks — the oceans, air, soil, and forests that store pollutants — are filling up. The world seemed boundless until recently. There seemed no obstacle to the developing world attaining the West's lifestyle and to everyone enjoying it indefinitely. We know more now. Time for a new plan.

3 Energy

Life until the eighteenth century was powered by renewables: wood, water, wind, and the sunlight that grew the food that fueled human and animal power. Flick on a switch today and you're likely drawing on a <u>fossil fuel</u> — oil, coal, or natural gas. The first powers our transportation, while the last two are burned to make most of our electricity. They're versatile, miraculously potent, and available in huge amounts. So what's not to like? Once again, scarcity and side effects.

As population and consumption rose, we drained the easily accessible supplies, especially noticeable with oil. This is why you're seeing pressure to tap oil that's riskier to get (in the deep waters of the Gulf of Mexico), that's located in protected areas (the Arctic National Wildlife Reserve), or that requires so much energy to process that there's little net gain (Canadian tar sands and American <u>shale</u> oil).

A train bringing coal to a power plant. It takes thousands of coal cars each day to make coal's share of U.S. electricity. That share has dropped from one-half to one-third since 2008 due to coal's pollution problems and cheaper natural gas supplies.

Peak oil *is the moment when the amount of oil we can pump begins to decline — long predicted but not yet reached since we keep finding new sources and new ways to extract it. Cheap supplies do seem to have peaked. Today's new unconventional energy supplies take much more money and energy to get and process than old ones.*

The heavy oil in Canada's tar sands is mixed with clay and sand, requiring much energy and hot water to separate it out and upgrade it to crude oil. The much fought-over Keystone XL Pipeline is designed to bring the oil to refineries along the Gulf Coast to be turned into gasoline and other fuels.

We love our cars. Cars run on gas. Gas comes from oil. We'll go to any lengths to get it.

Fossil fuels hold the energy trapped in millions of years of compressed plant and animal remains. Because they're finite, the worry has always centered on scarcity. New finds offer huge new supplies, but demand outside of the West has grown so large that scarcity is still an issue. Suddenly, though, it's been trumped by side effects.

Those side effects are many. The 2010 Deepwater Horizon oil spill off the Gulf Coast was the largest in U.S. history. Burning coal puts dangerous mercury and acid rain–causing sulfur into the air. But nothing tops the newly realized multipronged problems of climate change. Of all the fossil fuels, coal releases the most greenhouse gases. Burning natural gas releases fewer, the reason it's been thought to be a safe bridge fuel to carry us to a clean-energy future. New findings that natural gas operations leak methane — a much more powerful greenhouse gas than CO_2 — have cast doubt on its smaller carbon footprint. At the same time, **fracking** has dramatically increased its supply.

Fortunately, there are alternatives. There's enough wind, solar, and other renewable energy sources to meet our demand many times over. Enough sunlight falls on the Earth in an hour to make all the electricity we use in a year. We'll need to install many more solar and wind systems and upgrade our grids — the networks that distribute electricity — to move power from areas rich in sun and wind. We'll need better batteries for storing energy when the sun isn't shining and the wind isn't blowing. Solar takes up lots of space; wind turbines kill birds. We'll need fixes for these and other problems. Progress is being made on all these fronts. Texas, the top oil-producing state, is now the U.S. leader in wind power.

There are other non–fossil fuel sources. Hydroelectric power from dams uses falling water, such a good deal that we've tapped most available sources and have lately regretted the side effects of damming rivers. Nuclear power comes with staggering costs

Fracking: *Also called hydraulic fracturing, this process pumps water and chemicals into shale formations at high pressure to force out oil and natural gas.*
PRO: *It opens vast new energy supplies that are close to home.*
CON: *It uses toxic chemicals that are suspected to have contaminated drinking water; fracking itself requires large amounts of water. You can read industry's safety claims at ExxonMobil's website; the documentary GasLand gives a different view.*

Is power from the sun and wind only practical in the sunny Southwest or on windy coastlines? A 2013 Stanford University study showed that New York State could make all its electricity from wind and solar by 2030.

How the world's electricity is made (2010):

Coal: 40%

Natural gas: 22%

Hydroelectric: 16%

Nuclear: 13%

Oil: 5%

Renewables: 4%

and dangers: radioactive wastes, worries over making nuclear weapons, and safety, especially after a 2011 earthquake and tsunami caused radiation releases from reactors in Fukushima, Japan. Turning plants into biofuels sounds like the perfect solution, but some plants (such as corn) consume as much energy as the fuels give back. Algae, hydrogen, waves, tides, and geothermal power from the Earth's own heat are among other candidates still in the early stages.

Transitions between energy sources usually take decades, but we've never been so motivated before to hurry up. You're watching a race: can we find substitutes for fossil fuels before their effect on climate grows too great?

England—the birthplace of the coal-fueled Industrial Revolution—is now home to the London Array, the world's largest offshore wind farm, measuring ninety square miles, off the mouth of the Thames River.

4 Food

Population keeps climbing; the supply of farmland doesn't. Though malnutrition and starvation are still with us, massive famines predicted for the late twentieth century didn't arrive. Why? We learned how to make our finite farmland produce more food. The breakthroughs, known as the Green Revolution, gave us higher-yielding strains of grains and **GMOs**. Pesticides cut losses from insects. Refrigeration fought spoilage. Irrigation brought reliable water. We used natural gas to make fertilizers, vastly increasing supply. Thomas Malthus would be stunned.

Problems? Alas, the usual suspects. Scarcity of fresh water, accelerated by irrigation, has already reached many parts of the world. We're losing land to erosion — modern farming is hard on soil — and to roads and buildings for our growing population. When we plant crops to make biofuels like ethanol, we're subtracting from our food-producing acreage, using land to feed machines instead of people.

Side effects? Greenhouse gases are high on the list. Tractors, chemical fertilizers, irrigation pumps, freezers — all of these depend on fossil fuels, so much so that modern agriculture puts out more greenhouse gases than transportation does. Their effect on climate is boomeranging back on food production, with harvests threatened by rainfall disruptions,

GMOs: *Genetically modified organisms whose handpicked genes can help plants fight weeds, pests, and drought, and increase nutrients. Concerns include mutations, interbreeding between GMOs and wild populations, and ignorance of long-term effects on humans and the environment.*

To see the fossil fuels hidden in your burger, read Michael Pollan's New York Times *article "Power Steer."*

17

floods, and record droughts in the bread-baskets of Australia, Europe, and the United States. If the Green Revolution isn't sustainable, we won't have beaten Thomas Malthus after all.

Factory farming releases more than greenhouse gases. Its huge harvests come from monocultures — growing large numbers of the same thing in one place. This is highly efficient and keeps prices low. But because it invites losses from disease and pests, it requires large doses of pesticides for plants, antibiotics for animals, and a blind eye to animals' living conditions. The result is that our groundwater can contain pesticides and growth hormones. Nitrogen from fertilizers has given us dead zones in river deltas. Antibiotics in milk and meat have spawned drug-resistant infections, a major problem in hospitals.

A morsel of news about meat: meat-eating has tripled since 1970. This matters. It takes a large amount of grain and water fed to animals to make a much smaller amount of meat — an average ratio of seven to one. This is the reason that meat was a luxury in most of the world until lately. Today, we're feeding half our grain to animals, losing enough food in the bargain to feed billions for the sake of meat's flavor and protein. As the West's meat-heavy diet spreads, tropical forests are felled to increase land for grazing or growing animal feed, releasing huge quantities of greenhouse gases. Cheap meat — fast food's foundation — is cheap only if you leave out its true costs and consequences.

For the full story behind your chicken nuggets and Big Mac, check out the book Chew on This *by Eric Schlosser and Charles Wilson or the documentary* Food, Inc.

5 Climate

All of these issues intersect at climate, altering it and being altered by it in return.

Rising population and consumption, the coming of the car, changes in agriculture, and deforestation all combined to put enough greenhouse gases into the atmosphere to raise global air and water temperatures.

Graphs like this point strongly to climate change being <u>anthropogenic</u> — caused by humans.

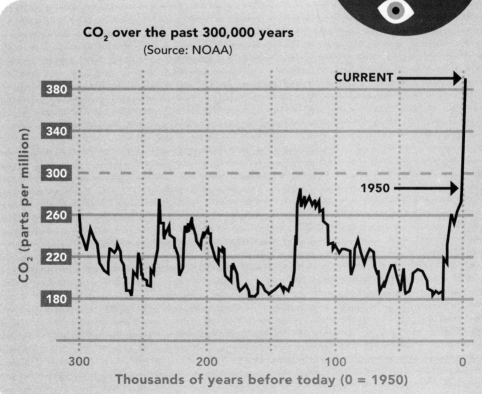

CO_2 over the past 300,000 years
(Source: NOAA)

CURRENT

CO_2 (parts per million)

380

340

300

1950

260

220

180

300   200   100   0

Thousands of years before today (0 = 1950)

Noticing

Scientists in the 1890s predicted this. The confirmations began showing up a century later, from spreading deserts to rising sea levels. Oceans absorbing increased CO_2 in the air have become more acidic. Extreme weather events predicted by models have become common. If we keep burning fossil fuels, we're headed for global disaster.

The good news: unlike an Earth-bound asteroid, we inadvertently made this problem and ought to be able to unmake it. The challenge: switching to green alternatives quickly enough. Fossil fuels permeate our lives. We'll need green sources for electricity to replace coal and natural gas, green fuels or electricity-powered transportation to replace oil, and a way to grow just as much food without fossil fuels. We've started down this path. Greenhouse gases already in the atmosphere will continue warming our climate for years. Bringing them down as low as we can as fast as we can is the best thing we can do for our future.

Climate is complex. Seawater can warm inconspicuously, but at 79°F it begins to promote hurricanes. There's a lot we don't know about such thresholds. The same goes for positive feedback loops that magnify effects, as when higher temperatures melt tundra, which releases methane, which raises temperature further. We used to think climate changed only slowly, but lately we've learned that it's swerved suddenly in Earth's past

The United Nations' Intergovernmental Panel on Climate Change (IPCC), the most authoritative body studying climate, assigns a 95–100 percent likelihood to humans' role in raising temperature, a view shared by the National Academy of Sciences, NASA, and the overwhelming majority of climatologists. There's plenty of debate about what might happen next, but virtually none among scientists on how we got here.

If we keep burning fossil fuels at current rates, we're on track to raise temperature 3.5 °F (2 °C) over pre-industrial levels around 2040. For what we can expect at each 1 °C rise, see Mark Lynas's book Six Degrees: Our Future on a Hotter Planet.

many times. Abrupt climate change is now a hot research topic.

What can we do? <u>Mitigation</u> (reducing the causes by cutting carbon emissions) and <u>adaptation</u> (preparing for the effects) have lately been joined by research in improving our situation through <u>geoengineering</u> projects like whitening clouds to reflect more of the sun's rays. We've raised temperature 1.4° since the start of the Industrial Revolution. Holding the increase to an additional three to four degrees will require major shifts at every level, from international bodies to individual households, and on all the issues flowing into climate.

Greenhouse gases, sea-level changes, and climate-related extinctions are anything but new. For the long view, check out J. D. Macdougall's book A Short History of Planet Earth: Mountains, Mammals, Fire, and Ice. *Then spring forward with Curt Stager's book* Deep Future: The Next 100,000 Years on Earth. *A seismic shift in your perspective is guaranteed.*

This book uses Fahrenheit (F), but Celsius (C) figures are common elsewhere, since scientists and nearly all other countries use that scale. A change of 1°C = 1.8°F. See the note to "We've raised temperature 1.4°" on p. 162.

For a powerful argument for keeping fossil fuels buried rather than burned, read Bill McKibben's 2012 article "Global Warming's Terrifying New Math" in *Rolling Stone*. The United Nations hopes to cap CO_2 levels at 450 parts per million (ppm), but others—like McKibben's group 350.org—feel we won't be safe unless we get it down to 350. The figure recently passed the 400 mark. You can find the latest reading at co2now.org.

my town
your town

Looking locally

Take the time to look — out the car window, in the newspaper, on websites covering what's happening in your area — and you'll likely pick out all the issues from the previous chapter. They're present even in my tiny town, Aromas, set in rolling hills ten miles from the Pacific. Here's what I see around me and slightly beyond:

THE MAJESTIC
Plastic Bag

0:24 / 4:00

Check out **The Majestic Plastic Bag** on YouTube, a witty four-minute mockumentary that turns the plastic bag problem inside out.

- Consumption generates trash: our landfill was almost full, causing the search for a replacement. To cut back on plastic trash, several local cities have passed restrictions on single-use plastic bags.

- Population has outgrown the freshwater supply. Two nearby coastal cities are debating desalinating seawater to get more.

- Farms need land. So do houses, businesses, schools, and roads. Several recent ballot measures have tried to protect farmland, a problem arising from population growth.

Noticing

Manhattan is America's greenest city? Read all about it—and a mind-boggling description of Phoenix's sprawl—in David Owen's hymn to high density, Green Metropolis.

Santa Cruz (CA) Sentinel, 9-12-12

Aromas Group Seeks Moratorium on Oil Drilling, Tighter Controls

- To gain jobs and a share of the West's enviable lifestyle, millions have left their homes in developing countries for Europe, Australia, and the United States. Many Aromas residents or their parents were born in Latin America.

- It's nine miles to my usual grocery store, thirty to my usual library, and farther to many Aromas residents' jobs. Country and suburban living takes lots of gas. It also takes lots of infrastructure—roads and water pipes and power lines and everything else needed for all that spread-out development.

- The need for more energy led to exploratory drilling in the area, drawing us into the national debate over fracking.

- Salmon numbers in recent years have been low enough that the fishing season has sometimes been canceled. Overfishing and damming streams for water storage are the most likely causes.

Santa Cruz (CA) Sentinel, 4-10-08

Salmon fishermen brace for another season of no fishing

24

- I see the fossil-fuel component in food every day: acres of plastic covering strawberry fields before planting, the night-time glow from greenhouses, and fleets of trucks taking local produce nationwide.

- A large crop of farmers' markets has sprung up in the region, showing public enthusiasm for alternatives to factory farming.

History is happening here and now. It's in our medicine cabinets, on our dining-room tables, and in the daily weather report. Now that we can make out the issues, let's see how we're dealing with them.

The Big Here quiz, brainchild of *Wired* magazine's Kevin Kelly, lets you check your own local knowledge. It's online at http://kk.org/helpwanted/archives/001084.php.

Perception

Perception

vested interests

Seeing behind headlines and talking heads

N

o tool in your mental kit
has more power to weigh
the worth of statements
or reveal the source of actions than the ability to
spot vested interests. These are the stakes — the
financial or emotional investment — we have in
an idea, a policy, a business, a political party.

If you owned an energy-drink factory,
your desire to make a profit would give you
a vested interest in opposing laws that would
keep your product out of school vending
machines. You'd no doubt belong to a **trade
group** that would hire **lobbyists** to fight
such laws. Your trade group would hire public
relations (PR) firms to improve the public's
opinion of energy drinks through ads, articles,
Facebook posts, tweets, and the "talking
heads" you see interviewed on TV news.
The information dispersed might or might
not be accurate. Its goal isn't truth but
promoting energy drinks.

This distinction is crucial.
Impartial investigators have
nothing to gain from their
particular findings. They test
and revise them in a continuing
quest for accuracy. This is
the model science follows.
Vested interests' prime goal is

A trade group
*represents an industry
as a whole.*

Lobbyists *try to
influence politicians
through persuasion and
campaign donations.
The "energy-drink lobby"
would be all the businesses
with a vested interest in
selling energy drinks.*

Galileo's
observation of the stars
and planets had no agenda
other than curiosity. What he saw
convinced him that the Earth circled
the sun, putting him in conflict with the
vested interests of the Catholic Church,
which held to the Bible's assertion that
the Earth was unmoving. Fearing his
views would undercut its power,
the Church forbid Galileo to
publish his work.

preserving their power, not seeking truth. The evidence is all around you. When powerful people or institutions are accused of misconduct — from army massacres and police brutality cases to clergy sex-abuse scandals and cyclist Lance Armstrong's use of performance-enhancing drugs — the first reaction is almost always to refute the charge, no matter how accurate. If truth is a threat to power, money, or reputation, there's a strong motive to cover it up.

"I want you all to stonewall it. Let them plead the Fifth Amendment, cover up or anything else. . . . We're going to protect our people if we can."

President Richard Nixon to his aides in 1973 at the height of the Watergate scandal. Sometimes stonewalling can go on for decades. The Turkish government still denies the genocidal campaign against its Armenian population one hundred years ago.

This makes it easier to sort truth from falsehood in the environmental debate. Whatever you read, see, or hear, consider the source. If you detect vested interests, look elsewhere for information. For more on this, see "How to Weigh Information," on page 154.

People know that statements coming from vested interests can't be trusted. We're aware that car dealers just want to sell us a car, the reason we're wary of their claims. Vested interests know we know this. Their solution: **front groups.** These inject industries' views into public discourse without revealing their source. Coming up with deceiving names for groups expressly to fool the public is an art the PR industry has perfected. You'll find these names at the bottoms of campaign fliers, beneath the pro and con arguments in voters' guides, and included in articles and blog posts to give support from seemingly unbiased sources. Who would guess that Citizens for Recycling First is a coal industry front group promoting the use of coal ash in industry? The Greening Earth Society sounds green, but it's *in favor* of CO_2 emissions. Sometimes whole movements use deceptive names, like the Wise Use land movement in the western United States, which you'd think would focus on long-range planning and protection. Instead, it promotes logging, mining, and property owners' rights to do what they want with their land. It's amazing how many ways we've figured out to lie.

Vested interests come in all shapes and sizes, from makers of bubblegum to nuclear bombs, each fighting for its corner of the economy. The fossil-fuel lobby is the biggest kid on the environmental block. Everybody needs energy. Selling coal, oil, and gas to so many buyers has made fossil-fuel suppliers immensely profitable. Do renewable power companies hire lobbyists, file lawsuits, fund **think tanks,** and try to shape public opinion?

Front group:
A group whose name is meant to hide who's behind it and what it's promoting. A front group's nightmare: having its funders revealed, as happened to the Heartland Institute in 2012. Companies selling fossil fuels, liquor, tobacco, and prescription drugs were among its supporters. For a long list of front groups and who they're hiding, go to http://www .sourcewatch.org/index .php/Front_groups.

Think tanks *produce papers on policy and usually pick names with a scholarly or neutral air. In truth, they speak for the industries who fund them.*

The top ten
corporations
on *Fortune*
magazine's
Global 500 list
for 2012:

1 **Royal Dutch Shell**

2 **ExxonMobil**

3 **Wal-Mart Stores**

4 **BP**

5 **Sinopec Group**

6 **China National Petroleum**

7 **State Grid**

8 **Chevron**

9 **ConocoPhillips**

10 **Toyota Motor**

Most definitely. But because they have so much less money to spend, their campaign is dwarfed in comparison.

To earn their profits, fossil-fuel businesses have invested trillions of dollars in oil rigs and supertankers, mines and gas stations, refineries and pipelines. If climate worries spur politicians to tax carbon emissions, push conservation, or speed a switch to other fuels, those trillions will earn back far less money and turn out to be a poor investment. They'd be as unhappy as you'd be if you spent big bucks on a laptop that died a month later.

Less money coming in means lower profits and less of all the things that money can buy, including power and respect. Somebody else will be at the top of the Fortune 500. Which brings us to something you've probably observed: people hate to lose power. This is as true on Wall Street and in Congress as it is in high-school cliques. Powerful interests fight to keep their standing. There are 535 members of Congress and an estimated two thousand Washington lobbyists working solely on climate legislation — roughly seventeen hundred of them representing fossil fuels. That works out to more than three lobbyists per politician fighting against reducing greenhouse gases, a sign of how much money is at stake. In place of the Catholic Church, many of today's scientists find themselves facing off against the fossil-fuel lobby, which is similarly powerful and determined not to give ground.

But science and technology cause the ground to keep shifting. The Pony Express was put out of business when the telegraph was invented. The telegraph was doomed by the telephone. Coachmakers, saddlers, stablers, harness-makers, and all the other trades connected to horses were sent into a tailspin by the coming of the car. Progress has losers as well as winners, and the losers aren't happy,

naturally enough. The new news on fossil fuels is pushing them in the direction of the horse — but they won't go without a fight.

This is the heart of the matter. We had no idea of fossil fuels' side effects for the first two centuries. No guilt there. But now we know. There's no excuse for continuing down this road, but the companies giving us these fuels don't want to sacrifice their massive investment. Understandable for them. Disastrous for us.

What might change this? Read on.

Producers of butter, which is made from cream, were threatened when vegetable-based margarine appeared. The powerful dairy lobby leaned on politicians and got many states to pass laws prohibiting margarine makers from adding yellow dye to make their white product resemble butter. Some laws even forced the addition of unappetizing pink dye.

common
sense

Seeing is believing— and limiting

volution equipped us to respond to threats: dangerous animals, flash floods, human attackers. Mortal danger grips us like no other subject. Why else are there so many crime shows on TV? Deadly beasts still rouse us, the reason the web teems with videos of attacks by everything from great white sharks to rabid squirrels. Yet environmental problems that could bring death and destruction produce yawns. Why?

Invisibility. You can see the charging grizzly with your naked eye. Not so cancer-causing microparticles in car exhaust or hormone-disrupting BPA on cash-register receipts. Cleverly, we add a rotten-egg scent to natural gas to alert us, but most of the human-made threats we've surrounded ourselves with fly under our sensory radar.

Distance. Polar ice might be melting, but it's far away from most of us. Our reaction to threats often varies with their nearness: the closer they are, the more seriously we take them. No wonder that residents of low-lying islands and coasts are

Seattle (WA) Examiner, 7-30-10

Store receipts are newest BPA toxin culprit— and at much higher levels

Perception

One of the places where climate change is most obvious is the Arctic, where few humans live. For the latest news and photos from that region, check out **arctic.noaa.gov,** maintained by the National Oceanic and Atmospheric Administration (NOAA).

far more panicked than the rest of the world about rising sea levels from global warming. Or that Hurricane Sandy in 2012 made many residents of New York and New Jersey believers in the destructive power of hurricanes. Sight is humans' dominant sense, but it illuminates only a tiny circle around us. Satellites, microscopes, TVs, and computers have worked recent wonders in overcoming this limitation.

Few of us have been to Newtok, on Alaska's west coast. For those who live there, climate change is big news: the Army Corps of Engineers estimates the village will be underwater in 2017.

Countering this trend is the small house movement. See the book *Tiny Homes: Simple Shelter* by Lloyd Kahn for a tour.

Joel Fleck
HOMEBUILDER
& RESIDENT
SEBASTOPOL

Time span. Changes with fluctuations (like climate) or that are gradual can go unseen. Few people noticed that the average U.S. house size doubled after 1950, demanding far more resources and fuel. Though they might not register, slow changes like this determine what we consider normal. If you're a fisherman who rarely sees a cod, this seems normal even though fifty years earlier cod were caught by the boatload. This is the problem called creeping normalcy or shifting baselines, which leaves us aware of changes within our lifetime but blind to longer-term developments. Photographs, paintings, and histories do important work in extending our view into the past.

The Old Weather project is seeking students to digitize data from uploaded logbooks of early visitors to the Arctic, increasing our knowledge of the region's past climate. This is just one of many citizen science projects sponsored by Zooniverse (**zooniverse.org**).

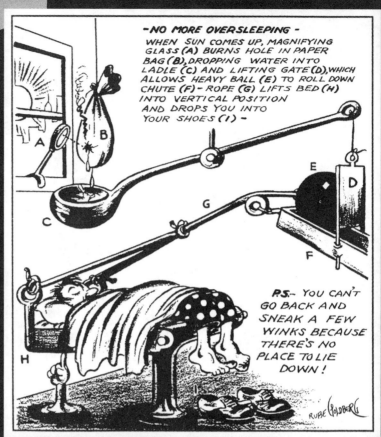

Cartoonist Rube Goldberg specialized in making simple processes wildly complex and meshed. Maybe he was actually right.

Complexity. Deforestation in Brazil is lowering rainfall in the U.S. Midwest. Midwest farming is causing fish in the Pacific to change their ranges. The connections are real but too complex to be obvious and inspire action. We like simple explanations that take the least time and mental effort — one reason stereotyping appeals to us. Unfortunately, we keep finding out how complicated the world's workings are. Our minds can give up when facing too much complexity. Or not, since we're also endowed with persistence.

Uncertainty.

We know that
Hurricane Katrina hit
New Orleans on August 29, 2005,
but was it worsened by global warming?
Facts are undeniable, but links between
them aren't. Science aims for increasingly
plausible explanations of those links, but
they're always open to challenge. This
leaves room for doubt. Rumors of the
health dangers of cell phones have
swirled for years, but how many of us
have stopped using them just to be
safe? Me neither. Uncertainty gives
us grounds for ignoring threats.

San Jose (CA) Mercury News, 6-1-11

Cellphones "possibly" linked to cancer, health panel says

Our senses are a narrow keyhole on the
world. Our brains are strongly inclined toward
the clear-cut even when situations are anything
but. Common sense is constantly praised but
it can sometimes lead us toward illusions. To
decode the world accurately, we all need to
correct for its biases and think outside its box.

out of sight

Why many adults don't know the facts of life

M

y sister once showed a Native American from Barrow, Alaska, around her area of California. When she pointed to some chickens at a farm they visited, he spoke the unforgettable line, "So *that's* what they look like." He'd only seen plastic-wrapped chicken parts in grocery stores.

We're all in the same situation, actually. It's hard to grasp the causes of environmental problems when so much information isn't in view. We might have walked into McDonald's hundreds of times, but how many of us have ever entered a slaughterhouse? You've got a cell phone, but have you stood in a lead mine, seen copper smelted, or watched oil turned into plastic? Why is so much about the things we buy out of sight?

City living. Most Westerners live

in cities, far from the mines, farms, forests, mills, refineries, and oil and gas fields where our products begin. Manufacturing that does happen in cities usually takes place in areas apart from residential neighborhoods.

If you do live close to where things are made, the health risks might make you wish you didn't. Environmental-justice complaints center on unequal exposure to pollution.

Fort Wayne (IN) Journal Gazette, 12-14-05

Minority, poor Hoosiers clustered near pollution

Globalization.

The drive to cut costs has moved many American jobs out of sight to other continents. With supplies coming from all corners of the globe, even products made close by have invisible pasts.

Specialization.

Having employees work on a single task instead of making an entire product is wonderfully efficient. One of the downsides: employees tend to know only a sliver of what goes on.

The same is true of specialization within societies. With only 2 percent of the U.S. population in agriculture, 98 percent of us never see our food being raised. We'll need to dig to get the information we're missing.

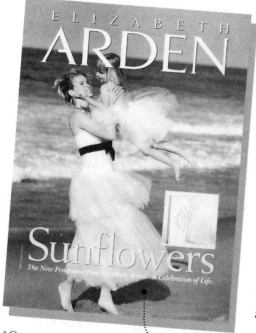

⤵ For a college student's quest to build a toaster from scratch, including making iron into steel in a microwave, see Thomas Thwaites's entertaining talk at **ted.com.**

Advertising.

Look closely at ads and you'll notice how rarely they show a product before it's for sale or after it's thrown away. If we saw the oil slicks and child labor that lie behind some of our purchases, we might think twice — the reason ad images are fun-filled, soothing, and often set in an earlier era. In Adland, the air is unpolluted, families are close, and people are often in a state of elation.

The media. TV and radio stations, magazines, and newspapers all survive by selling ads. This gives them a vested interest in avoiding confronting the public with unpleasant truths about their purchases. A few sources, like the TV show *60 Minutes,* serve an audience that expects muckraking — journalism that exposes troubling facts. The vast majority of media outlets are owned by large corporations with a stake in the economy as a whole, giving them a motive to serve as cheerleaders for consumption and our current lifestyle. Would aliens monitoring American prime-time TV ever guess we're facing a major crisis?

Concealment. You've eaten *how* many hot dogs but never seen a hog become a sausage? No surprise there. Those images would be a further PR disaster for the meat industry, which has been embarrassed by secretly recorded videos showing abusive treatment of animals at farms and slaughterhouses. Information is precious and therefore often locked away. The small amounts on food and drug labels — from the suicide risks of antidepressants to the growth hormones in milk — had to be fought for by consumer groups for decades. That battle continues in the struggle to get food labels to include the presence of GMOs, fiercely opposed by biotech, agribusiness, and grocery interests. Some facts aren't too far away, but are purposely hidden.

"I find television very educating. Every time somebody turns on the set, I go into the other room and read a book."

Groucho Marx, American comedian

Batavia (NY) Daily News, 6-9-11

Bill would ban secret videotaping at farms

To help extract oil and gas from rock, fracking fluid contains solvents, friction reducers, and other toxic substances. In 2005, former vice president Dick Cheney — previously CEO of the drilling company Halliburton — pushed for an energy bill clause that allowed drillers to keep their fracking ingredients secret. Worries over contaminated drinking water have led several states to pursue closing the "Halliburton loophole."

With our experience so limited and our media so distorted a mirror, it's not surprising that nearly three-quarters of Americans in one survey had no idea that plastic comes from oil. Oddly, one of the few times that the facts of life are revealed is during disasters — when the public's right to know outweighs vested interests' ability to hide and we're given a brief look at the true costs of our lifestyle.

Reporters after the Deepwater Horizon oil spill, the first time many Americans learned anything about deepwater oil drilling. *E. coli* outbreaks have shone a light on our inadequate food safety system. The 9/11 attacks exposed our stumbling intelligence agencies along with the dangerous substances in our buildings that led to the toxic dust many inhaled.

You don't have time to wait around for a mine collapse? Here are some other ways to find the facts.

Education. The Internet has caused such a surge in documentaries that a search on nearly any topic will likely bring up a film. Other resources:

- The Worldwatch Institute offers profiles of common products from soap to cell phones. Search for "Good Stuff" at its website.

- The Story of Stuff website has animated films on electronics, bottled water, and cosmetics along with lots of print information on consumption issues.

Ratings. Since companies' vested interests make their own claims suspect, you need someone else—a third party—to investigate environmental and labor practices and to see through **greenwashing.**
Here are some that are doing just that:

- Goodguide.com rates products.

- Climatecounts.org rates companies.

- The Skin Deep Cosmetics Database at Environmental Working Group's website (ewg.org) rates personal care products.

- Foods labeled "Fair Trade" or "Organic" have been certified for their sustainable practices.

What about when there aren't any good choices? Time for government to step in. Taxes, regulation, research funding, and safety standards are some of the ways governments change what's available. They don't usually act without prodding. See the chapters "Democracy" (page 74) and "Fixes" (page 136).

In 1800 in Britain, the product was sugar and the downside was slave labor. Showing consumers the cruelty they were funding was a big part of the campaign that brought an end to slavery in the British Empire. Read all about it in the book *Sugar Changed the World: A Story of Magic, Spice, Slavery, Freedom, and Science* by Marc Aronson and Marina Budhos.

Greenwashing—
the eco-version of whitewashing—is a company's attempt to look greener than it is. It's no coincidence that green packaging has sprung up everywhere.

in the
now

The future feels unreal, until it's the present

No Payments Due for One Year

GET IT NOW, FREE!

BUY NOW, PAY LATER!

W e reacted at once to the attack on Pearl Harbor. The same with 9/11. But the environmental peril is different — a calamity that's mainly in the future. How does that affect things?

Evolution focused our eyes on the present. The first priority is the predator on your heels, not the one that hasn't been born. Future threats, especially if they unfold in slow motion like this one, don't shoot adrenaline into our veins.

Look around and you'll see how poorly we judge when the future will become the present, even with events that we *know* will occur. We have a full year to prepare for Christmas, yet stores are filled with last-minute shoppers on December 24. Post-office lines stretch out the door on April 15, the deadline for mailing tax returns. It's always later than we think — the reason some people set their clocks slightly ahead. Despite this trick, along with sticky notes and calendars synced to our phones, the future often catches us unaware.

The result is a mad scramble to catch up. With the environment, the difference between preventing now and scrambling later is huge.

Don't worry about the environment — it'll go away

The 2006 Stern Review, commissioned by the British government, estimated that dealing with climate change later would cost up to twenty times more than addressing it now. Politicians took the findings seriously. Two years later, the U.K. passed its landmark Climate Change Act.

Check out the Long Now Foundation for a group devoted to extreme long-term thinking and projects, including the building of a ten thousand–year clock.

Picture an orderly fire drill, then a real fire's desperate panic. Now multiply until you're at the scale of cities, then countries. So why aren't we doing more?

Remember the pleasure-loving grasshopper and the farsighted ant in Aesop's fable? We're both. We can plan ahead and avert problems. Agriculture gave us food surpluses that were wisely stored against future crop failures. We staff fire departments against threats that haven't yet occurred. Twentieth-century China and Bangladesh foresaw population catastrophes and worked at lowering their growth rates. The Dutch plan for adapting to climate change looks two hundred years ahead. But our inner grasshopper's voice is strong. *Spending all Saturday on a term paper that isn't due for a week?* Enduring discomfort in the present to avoid it in the future is usually a tough sell.

Normalcy bias — "It's never happened to me so why worry?" — comes into play here. If we've suffered because of some choice we've made, that experience is a powerful motivator for avoiding it in the future. This is why behavior that seems harmless to teens can feel wildly risky to parents; adults have likely paid the price in their pasts or know someone who has. Many cultures have folktales about a child who doesn't know the value of fear. In the case

"Once bitten, twice shy."

Saying

of global warming, we're all like that child. None of us has lived through a 5° temperature rise, so the threat feels unreal.

Placing environmental problems in the hazy future is one way to make them go away. When the downsides show up in the present, you get headlines like this. These events aren't ahead of schedule; we're behind, as usual.

Politicians often appeal to the grasshopper in us, knowing we prefer putting off worry and action. What they and we forget is that today's long-distance problems become tomorrow's present ones. You'll hear leaders speak of acting on behalf of their grandchildren, but when spending or sacrifices are proposed with the future in mind, resistance is fierce on behalf of the present. The unborn don't vote, hire lobbyists, or lead protests, and it shows; they, like future threats, go on our brain's back burner.

In bad economic times, our view shortens even more. We're focused on the next rent payment and the next gas fill-up. This makes sense. You have to survive the present to get to the future. But what do we do if our present needs — for a thriving economy built on high consumption and energy use — conflict with our long-term interests? When the present and future battle, the present nearly always wins. Here's our challenge: making both of them livable.

Christian Science Monitor, 5-3-07

Arctic Melt-off ahead of Schedule

"The best time to plant a tree is twenty years ago. The second-best time is now."

Chinese proverb

BACKSTORY:
THE OIL EMBARGO

How 1973 brought us hatchbacks, Sony TVs, and Alaskan oil

I
It began with a surprise attack on Yom Kippur, the holiest Jewish holiday. Israeli forces were driven back by the armies of Egypt and Syria and ran low on arms. The emergency airlift President Nixon approved helped turn the tide for Israel but brought retaliation in the form of an embargo: the Arab countries stopped selling their oil to the United States, Europe, and Japan. The war ended shortly, but the embargo went on for five months. You can still see its effects.

Only about one-tenth of U.S. oil came from the Middle East, but this was enough to cause blocks-long lines for gas pumps in some states. The government asked stations to close on Saturday nights and Sundays, then asked drivers with odd-numbered license plates to buy gas only on odd-numbered days. Because some electricity was made by burning oil, there were no lights on the White House Christmas tree that year. The Arab members of the Organization of the Petroleum Exporting Countries (OPEC) raised prices steeply, creating the first oil crisis for the West. How did nations respond?

- **The United States.**
  Highway speed limits
  went down to the
  more energy-efficient
  55 miles per hour.
  Average car mileage
  was 13 miles per
  gallon; the govern-
  ment demanded that
  Detroit double that in
  ten years, which it did.
  Smaller and lighter
  hatchback cars, already
  popular in Europe,
  spread to the United
  States. Desperate to
  increase domestic oil
  no matter how difficult
  to transport, Congress
  approved building
  the Alaskan oil pipe-
  line. We promoted coal
  and natural gas for
  electricity and began
  storing emergency
  oil in underground
  caverns in Texas and
  Louisiana, something
  we're still doing.

- **Japan** has virtually no oil and was completely dependent on the Middle East. It encouraged less energy-intensive industries like electronics, leading to decades of dominance. Its automotive industry was already making small, fuel-efficient cars and light trucks; suddenly it had a huge new market in the United States, where Toyotas and Datsuns became wildly popular, dealing Detroit a blow that's still being felt.

- **Europe's** governments raised taxes on gas and larger car engines to cut oil imports. Britain exploited its North Sea oil. Denmark pursued wind power, in which it's now a leader. France invested in nuclear power, the source of most of its electricity today.

Oil well fires burn in Kuwait near a destroyed Iraqi tank during the Gulf War (1990–1991).

Demands for energy independence were heard again in 1979–1980 when the revolution in Iran and the Iraq-Iran war cut oil exports sharply. President Jimmy Carter repeated President Nixon's calls to conserve. Reacting to the Soviet Union's 1979 invasion of Afghanistan, he declared that America would defend its vital interests in the Persian Gulf with force, a vow made good by later presidents in the Gulf War (1990–1991) and Iraq War (2003–2011).

New technology has given the United States access to new oil supplies at home, putting it among the world's leading producers and trimming our reliance on the Middle East. Still, you can hear the echo of 1973 in calls to build the Keystone XL pipeline and to drill in the Arctic National Wildlife Refuge. You can see it in the generous government subsidies still being given to oil and gas companies. You can find it as well in the words of U.S. politicians, who regard talk of conservation as taboo. The images of angry drivers waiting for gas haven't lost their power.

Defense

Mechanisms

denial

Problem? What problem?

Nobody likes bad news. It causes doubt and fear. The psychology pioneer Sigmund Freud was the first to describe how we use defense mechanisms to ward off uncomfortable feelings. You'll see several in action on the environmental front.

Denial is often the first line of defense: refusing to accept that the bad news is true. Patients diagnosed with a terminal disease may be soothed by denial. Drink-until-they-drop alcoholics can convince themselves that they don't have a problem. No matter how high the mountain of evidence, denial can make it vanish.

The deluding voices don't always come from inside us. They can be supplied from outside — the form of denial that's prominent in the debate over climate change. When the news on climate began appearing in the 1980s, the fossil-fuel lobby saw the threat to its interests and began work on disconnecting their product from global warming in the public's mind. Former vice president Al Gore's documentary *An Inconvenient Truth* made the case for that connection to the general public in 2006, rousing a large segment of the country. Since then, the lobby has

For a look at the denial machine in motion, check out the "Climate of Doubt" episode of the TV show *Frontline*, streaming at **http://www.pbs.org /wgbh/pages/frontline /climate-of-doubt.**

See **skepticalscience.com** for a constantly updated list and discussion of the arguments used against global warming.

hit back hard, determined to block or delay laws, taxes, and regulations that would cost it money. Its strategy toward politicians: lobbying. Toward the public who elects those politicians: actively encouraging denial. Here are some techniques you'll notice.

Sowing doubt.
The vast majority of climate scientists believe global warming is real, a serious threat, and caused by humans, but fossil-fuel interests have painted the issue as undecided and hotly debated. They have the clout to demand that their viewpoint be heard on TV, in newspapers, on radio, and in school textbooks.

Creating support.
The lobby funds its own legitimate-sounding research institutes to produce desirable statistics and passes money through front groups to scientists who support denial. Some of these are unqualified junk scientists who are paid to cast doubt on the carbon-climate connection.

Hiding sources. Front groups are a key part of the campaign; if Exxon published books and its executives were interviewed on talk radio, the claims would be rejected as obviously self-interested. A new wrinkle in concealment is the creation of **Astroturf groups** to give the appearance of **grassroots** support. To further spread their views but hide their source, fossil-fuel companies have paid PR firms to produce video features on energy and climate that have been slipped into TV news broadcasts without mentioning their source. Secrecy reigns in the funding realm as well. Though some fossil-fuel companies now state that global warming is real and caused by humans, they continue to channel millions of dollars to the denial campaign through anonymous donations.

Noted physicist Freeman Dyson is the most respected of those scientists who find global warming claims overblown. You can find his views in an interview at **e360.yale.edu.**

Grassroots:
Growing spontaneously out of popular opinion.

Astroturf groups *look like the real thing but are secretly orchestrated by a lobby trying to pass off its views as the public's. For more, see the documentary (Astro)Turf Wars.*

Spreading calm.

People can tell something's up with the weather. The record-breaking heat waves, floods, and droughts are too big to deny. In place of fossil fuels, the energy lobby has offered the comfort of nonhuman causes: sunspots, natural cycles, or the claims that climate isn't changing or is actually cooling.

The 2011 floods in Australia covered an area larger than France and Germany combined.

The jobs card. Every magician knows the power of misdirection — getting the audience to look left so as not to notice what you're doing on the right. Remember this when you notice industries associating their products with something unrelated but positive. The gun lobby and the health-insurance lobby can't publicly shout that they're fighting for profits, so they've tied their causes to Americans' love of freedom, getting the public to help push their fight to block reform. For the fossil-fuel lobby, the distracting lure has been jobs. Recasting the energy debate as New Jobs vs.

No Jobs conveniently leaves fossil fuels' big-time problems out of the picture, along with the jobs that renewables create. It's a tactic that keeps our eyes on the present and averted from the future. You'll often see it used negatively, with environmental regulations labeled as job killers. With unemployment high, the jobs card is more effective than ever, the reason it's played so often.

Sprinkling fairy dust.

A slogan like "Clean Coal" (from carbon capture and other proposals) magically solves the many problems of the dirtiest fossil fuel. The words might seem to express a wish for **carbon capture and storage,** but by equating "coal" with "clean," they encourage the fantasy that we can keep burning coal without suffering side effects. Coal companies have funded a major campaign to popularize this denial-promoting slogan.

Carbon capture and storage (CCS) *would liquefy CO_2 from coal-burning power plants' emissions and bury it underground, a process still in the testing stage.*

Discrediting alternatives.

Fossil fuels came with challenges and costs. Engineers, geologists, and chemists worked for decades to solve the problems behind fracking and deepwater drilling, aided by billions in federal aid. Renewables come with challenges as well, but you may already have noticed the PR campaign painting wind and solar as impractical and ruinously expensive.

CLEAN COAL

"They only work when the sun shines and the wind blows" is the most common line, sown throughout the media and repeated by politicians. The statement is true but leaves out a lot: our ability to store power from these sources, the fact that sun and wind don't decline in quality and quantity as coal and oil supplies have, and the overwhelming cost savings of not disrupting climate.

Scores of books and articles have been written accusing the fossil-fuel lobby of deliberate misinformation. Since the denial effort is essentially an ad campaign, it shouldn't surprise us to see half-truths and advertising's other tools at work. Its methods were developed decades earlier by the tobacco industry, which was similarly desperate to avoid government regulation and to assure the country that its product was safe. Discrediting scientists and buying friendly research were tactics used as well by chemical companies fighting calls to ban the pesticide DDT in the 1960s. Those efforts failed. This one has triumphed, dramatically turning a large slice of the American public against action on climate.

What explains this success? Why would underdog-loving Americans help the world's richest

corporations maintain their profits? Perhaps it's the size of the campaign this time around, with denial pouring out of every communication channel from books to e-mail to TV to tweets. Perhaps it's the fact that the link between fossil fuels and climate is harder for the public to see and accept than the one between tobacco and cancer.

Political polarization has played a role as well. The United States is divided into liberal (Democratic) and conservative (Republican) camps, with a bundle of positions that go with membership in either. Up into the 1990s, there was broad support for tackling climate among Republicans. To protect themselves, vested interests worked hard thereafter to make climate denial one of the views that all Republicans held. Politicians who needed those interests' money had a major motive to fall in line, and people

The 2012 Republican candidates for president included Jon Huntsman, who declared his belief in human-caused climate change—and was condemned by his rivals and trounced by Republicans in the primary elections.

tend to believe what they hear from their own party, especially if it's reinforced by the media.

So here we are. What might help? Mandatory critical thinking classes? Giving candidates free TV ads to get some of the money out of politics? It's a challenge awaiting your never-before-thought-of ideas.

projection

The lure of blaming others

 **GREEN IS THE NEW RED**

Rome (GA) News-Tribune, 4-27-03

Environmentalism Actually Is the Enemy of Human Life

Grand Junction (CO) Free Press, 10-26-09

Radical Environmentalists Undermine Human Progress

Criticism stings. We dislike hearing anything negative about our values or actions. *We're* the bad guy? Mental sirens blare, rousing us to fight the charges.

Accepting criticism is hard, the reason it's considered a mark of maturity. Individuals like to see themselves as flawless. The defense mechanism projection helps maintain that illusion. With one swift move it turns the tables on critics, dismissing their claims by projecting the negative behavior onto them. They, not we, are the real problem.

You can see this in action when environmentalists are described in ways that incite fear about them rather than about the dangers we're courting. "Radical" is a favorite fear-inducing adjective. Those who've filmed animal abuse at factory farms and slaughter-houses have been termed terrorists. Environmental regulations and carbon-cutting measures are routinely described as job-killers.

A few environmental groups, like the Earth Liberation Front, have indeed earned fear-stoking terms by using arson and sabotage against development, SUV dealerships, and other targets.

While denial tries to discredit opponents, projection demonizes them, taking
the anxiety that their message stirs in us
and converting it into aggression. If you
don't like the news, projection lets you take
it out on the bearer. "Shooting the messenger" is the ultimate in projection.

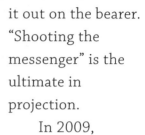

**REDUCE CARBON EMISSIONS--
SHOOT AN ENVIRONMENTALIST**

In 2009,
hackers released e-mails from climatologists and claimed that these proved scientists were manipulating data to support
their global-warming opinions. This became
known as Climategate. It was a classic projection maneuver, reversing the usual claim that
fossil-fuel companies distort findings to back
up the conclusions they desire. The several
investigations into the affair acquitted the
scientists, but that was months after they'd
been tarred in the media. With projection,
as with political mudslinging, he who flings
first often wins. The aim is to supply people
with a reason to reject claims without exam-
ining them.

As news worsens, more effort is needed
to exclude and deny it. This requires tightly
closed eyes and minds. Those who don't
criticize but merely point to the facts may be
attacked as doom-and-gloomers, alarmists,
or traitors. We've reached this stage in the
United States, where TV meteorologists who

connect weather events to global warming risk alienating viewers and losing their jobs.

One of projection's lures is that it places the enemy outside of us. A foreign threat is a powerful motivator, uniting and energizing nations in wartime. This is one reason leaders in trouble often blame other countries or pick wars, redirecting discontent abroad. The lack of a despised villain makes the environmental cause harder to get behind. Our threats can't be addressed without admitting our responsibility — something our minds are built to resist. Will floods and hurricanes and droughts fill in for foreign enemies and inspire our best efforts? Stay tuned.

"Be a good weather bimbo and stick to pointing out high pressure systems — and shut up about climate change."

Heidi Cullen, former climatologist for The Weather Channel, describing readers' reaction to her blog post arguing that TV meteorologists have a responsibility to educate the public about climate change.

A poster from the first Earth Day, 1970. Cartoonist Walt Kelly's line plays off of Commodore Perry's "We have met the enemy and he is ours" from the War of 1812.

regression

The joys of
childishness

Teenagers get criticized for not acting their age — putting off chores, ignoring consequences, acting impulsively. The shocking truth: adults probably have them beat. With the daunting issues facing us, it's easy to see the appeal of retreating to a childlike stage without responsibility. This is the defense mechanism <u>regression</u>. Where can you see it?

Credit cards. You haven't saved enough money but you really want something now? Go ahead and buy it anyway!

Tax revolts. Maturity demands looking beyond our narrow interests. Contributing to the public good from our private pockets causes some adults to throw tantrums. ....●

Shootings. Don't like your boss/ex-wife/gum-chewing coworker? Blowing them away is a childish fantasy with such appeal that some mentally unstable people act it out.

What's the link to the environment? Regression encourages the childish belief that our wishes can be fulfilled magically, without costs. We can have riches without work and wars without tax increases.

"If you really want something in this life, you have to work for it. Now quiet, they're about to announce the lottery numbers!"

Homer Simpson

The makers of the Chinese online game Fantasy Westward Journey claim to have 29 million daily active users, far more than any other such game.

But solving environmental issues requires looking straight at reality and calculating the costs of our lifestyle and options. People under the spell of regression, by contrast, lean toward fantasy and avoidance. They don't climb back into cribs but often into artificial realms — TV, video games, sports fandom, shopping, social media.

I confess it: I read the sports section first. We all know the lure of tuning out reality for a time. But commitment to fantasy worlds has deepened to the point that more and more of us are becoming tourists rather than citizens in the real world. Surveyed Americans know more about the Simpson family than about the Constitution. Cable TV providers, movie studios, and video-game makers are more than happy to encourage our desire to escape.

The taller the challenge, the more tempting regression is. This explains the "elephant in the room" tendency to ignore big issues. We close our eyes to the elephant *because* it's enormous — so big that it's too large to deal with. This is why inaction is a common reaction to the environmental situation. Of all our options, going on as before is the easiest. To have nothing required of us except playing with our toys is the paradise regression offers.

Denial, projection, regression . . . and you thought your brain was your friend. Fortunately, we're not all under the sway of defense mechanisms. Large numbers of people see the issues before us and are taking action. Let's look at how our political and economic systems are responding.

Check out TV comic Jay Leno's "Jaywalk" segments in which he tests people's general knowledge. YouTube has high-school versions of the same.

To put the brakes on global warming, a research team at Princeton University concluded we'd need to accomplish eight fixes from the list of fifteen at **http://cmi.princeton .edu/wedges/intro.php.** All are big: increase fuel efficiency in 2 billion cars to 60 mpg; decrease the number of car miles by half; expand solar-powered electricity one hundred-fold; double current nuclear power; end tropical deforestation.

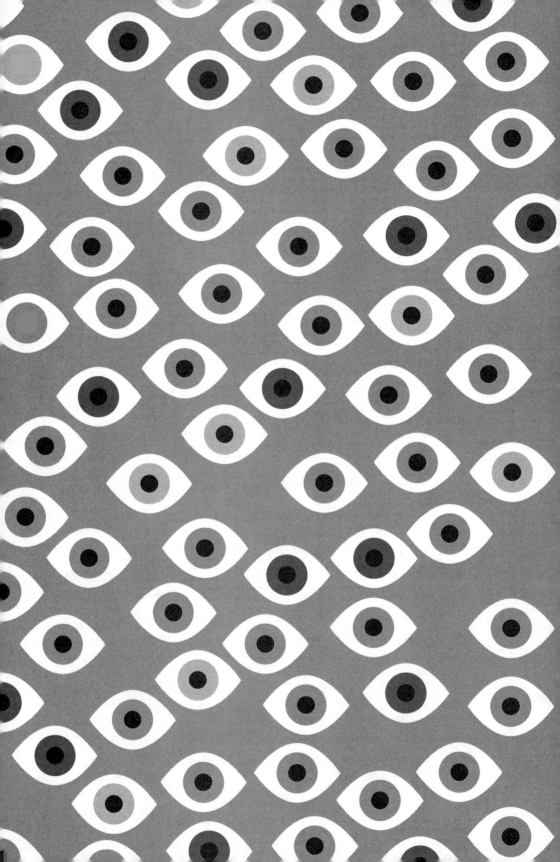

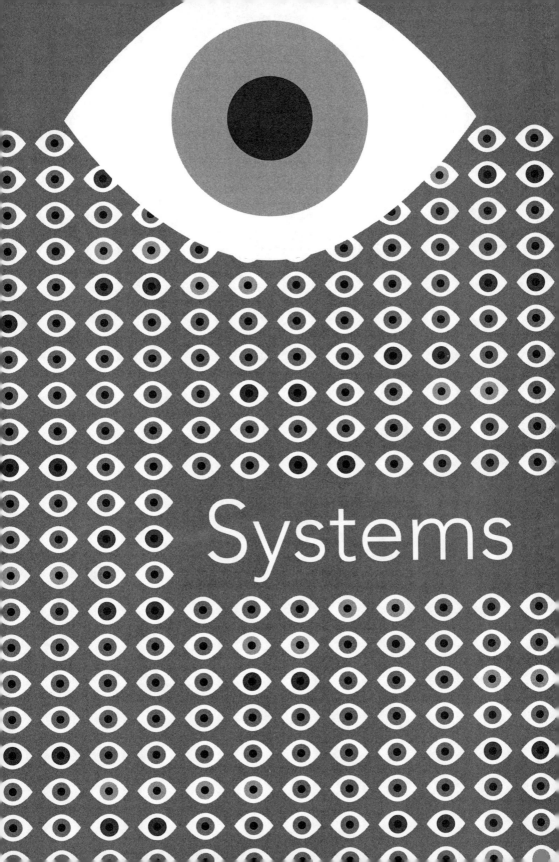

Systems

democracy

The pluses and problems of people power

I n Greek, *demos* means "people" and *kratia* means "power." To win elections, candidates have to please the people. This has both advantages and drawbacks.

Hard truths. Since people dislike bad news, especially if they share the blame, democracies are disadvantaged by a crisis like ours. Speaking unwelcome news can bring defeat. President Carter found this out in 1979, when worry over oil supplies led him to urge Americans to drive less and lower thermostats. The public was stunned by his gloomy frankness, a factor in his defeat the next year.

Politicians took note. No more requesting sacrifice. You'll also notice how rarely they ask voters to take responsibility for problems and how often they heap blame on Washington instead. Fear of offending voters can lead politicians to tell people what they want to hear instead of what they need to know. This need to please has led virtually the entire Republican party to deny human-caused global warming. The subject has become so taboo in many quarters that it was news when President Barack Obama spoke the words "climate change" in his 2013 State of the Union address. Since much of the country

Jimmy Carter described the energy crisis of the 1970s in terms of war, as a national threat that made conservation vital. The campaign flopped.

"I have nothing to offer but blood, toil, tears, and sweat."

Winston Churchill on becoming British prime minister during World War II. Some leaders have spoken the truth and survived. The difference in this case: Churchill's listeners knew they were in a fight to the death, while many Americans today believe the war is a mirage.

prefers the comforts of denial, projection, and regression, we haven't yet made great progress in facing our problems.

Responsiveness.

Leaders want to stay in power. Because of this, democracy can also respond well to crises. When the 1969 Santa Barbara oil spill and the first Earth Day a few months later brought loud calls for federal environmental safeguards, President Richard Nixon — not known as a tree hugger — created the Environmental Protection Agency (EPA) and went on to sign landmark laws protecting air, water, and endangered species. If enough voters demand hard truths, swift action, and long-term thinking, leaders are motivated to comply.

President Nixon signing the Clean Air Act in 1970. Today's environmentalists are trying to include greenhouse gases among the pollutants the act regulates. If they're successful, the EPA could push carbon producers to lower their emissions.

Speed.

Where quick action is needed, dictatorships have the edge — the reason armies aren't democracies. China's 1979 one-child policy for urban couples was decreed, not publicly debated for decades. It's made a difference in halting China's population growth, but it was also unpopular, evaded, and may soon be abolished. Democracies are slower, but having the public's consent can count for a lot.

Business influence. Money talks, they say. In politics, it shouts. American election campaigns are long and waged mainly with TV ads, which are very expensive. This requires candidates to raise millions, which leads them to the corporations that can afford the big donations needed to buy those ads. In return, business interests gain unprecedented influence on policies. They write legislation, shape politicians' positions, and suggest business-friendly appointments to committees and judgeships. Many attempts at reform over several decades have failed.

Innovation. The ability to vote and participate in politics encourages initiative and innovation in democratic societies. These traits have more opportunity when there are many different governments who might give new ideas a try. Christopher Columbus took his plan to ruler after ruler before finding a taker; had Europe been united, he might have had just one chance. The American federal system offers fifty different platforms for experimentation, along with countless cities. Good ideas are quickly copied, refined, and passed on. When Washington lags instead of leads, states and cities will often take the initiative, as many have in preparing for the effects of climate change.

Secrecy hides much of business interests' role in law-making. The American Legislative Exchange Council—out of public view until 2012—brings business executives and state legislators together to draft laws that industries would like to see passed, from limiting safety regulations to barring consumer lawsuits, and then introduces them in state houses. Watch it happen in journalist Bill Moyers's documentary The United States of ALEC.

SENATORS Should Wear Uniforms like Nascar Drivers so we could Identify their Corporate Sponsors

You can type in your representatives' names and see who's funding them at **opensecrets.org.**

Innovations' birthplaces: Curbside newspaper recycling: Madison, Wisconsin, 1968. Law requiring deposits on glass bottles: Oregon, 1971.

capitalism

The market knows best. Or does it?

You might not be able to vote yet, but your voice is heard in the economy. With companies vying for your dollars, the ones whose products fill the most need, have an edge in performance, and cost less than the competition will thrive. This is the promise of the **free market** — ever-improving quality at the lowest possible price. Every year, a dollar spent on a computer gets you more speed and memory than the year before. Capitalism's successes are all around us. Capitalism's problems surround us as well. How do they impact the environment? What solutions are being tried?

Keeping costs low. We all want
low prices, until you realize that the pressure to keep prices low motivates companies to avoid spending money on dealing with the pollutants and other environmental problems they cause. That money would require higher prices, which would make the company's products less competitive, hurting sales and profits. The same goes for spending more to buy raw materials from responsible suppliers, paying workers better, and making factories safer. This is the <u>race to the bottom</u>, the quest to reduce costs that's led many U.S. firms to move abroad where labor is cheaper and rules on working conditions and environmental safety are much

The **free market** *relies on consumers, not governments, to decide what products get made and how much they cost. Completely free markets are nonexistent, since all governments have seen the need to tax imported goods, restrict monopolies, set minimum wages, or otherwise intervene.*

For a look at what's behind rock-bottom prices, check out the documentary **Wal-Mart: The High Cost of Low Price.**

less strict. In this race, the one who exploits employees and the environment the most heartlessly wins.

What can be done? Unions came into being to protect workers. What about protecting bees and oceans? Governments can step in on their behalf — often prodded by citizen groups — and restrict the market's negative impacts. Through laws and regulations, governments can protect wild spaces, limit dangerous chemicals, rule on animal treatment, and set worker safety standards.

What can buyers do? First, recognize how low prices get so low and consider whether price is a product's most important feature. Second, know who you're giving your money to, something that's getting easier. The chapter "Out of Sight" (page 40) gives resources that will help you choose.

Huffington Post, 5-10-13

Bangladesh Factory Collapse: Death Toll Climbs Past 1,000

Protection varies. Does your lipstick contain lead, a neurotoxin? Are there carcinogens in your shampoo? European laws ban hundreds of chemicals considered dangerous; the U.S. Food and Drug Administration (FDA), hobbled by business interests, has banned only a handful. All cosmetics tested on animals were banned in the European Union in 2013.

The profit motive.

A tropical forest keeps CO_2 out of the atmosphere, gives us oxygen to breathe, reduces soil erosion, and fosters the diversity that makes an ecosystem resilient. Because these ecosystem services are free and scarcely noticed, they aren't valued — until they're missed, like the pollination of U.S. crops by native insects. We now know that our survival depends on them. And yet bulldozing a forest to graze cattle for meat or raise palm trees for oil makes perfect economic sense as our system stands.

Profits and the market aren't infallible guides. They've pushed innovation and given us dazzling products. They've also driven extinctions, the uprooting of half the world's tropical and temperate forests, and the filling of land, sea, and air with pollutants because there was no immediate financial price.

Once a crisis makes nature's value obvious, it takes government to change market-driven behavior. China did this in 1998, banning logging after decades of deforestation led to disastrous floods. There's now growing discussion about calculating the dollar value of ecosystem services and weighing it against the income from development.

Monocultures of palm trees, their oil used for cooking and in biofuel, have replaced tropical forests in many parts of the Southern Hemisphere, releasing CO_2, reducing diversity, and bringing erosion and pollution problems.

Misleading prices.

If prices reflected the actual environmental costs of products, what would happen? Gasoline would include the price of seawalls holding back rising oceans. Conventionally grown produce using synthetic fertilizers and pesticides would outprice organic after paying to clean up polluted water. Coal-fired electricity's price tag would include paying for damage caused by the spread of deserts and warm-weather diseases, making solar and wind energy cheap by comparison. Currently, businesses **externalize** those costs, letting the victims or government programs pay the bills. Prices that are lower than they ought to be fail to send signals that what's being bought is scarce or causes expensive side effects. This leaves society driving blindly.

One possible solution is to tax companies' environmental damage. Another is transparency — full disclosure of practices that would reward responsible businesses. Awareness of the triple bottom line — not just price, but social and environmental impacts — is becoming more common in the corporate world. Some businesses have been willing to make serious efforts at reducing harm. The more we support them, the stronger the signal we send back their way.

Externalize: *To shift costs outside of a business. Before Oregon's bottle bill, the beverage industry didn't have to spend money on redemption programs to deal with the problem of discarded bottles. That's still true in the states not listed on the label, where the beverage lobby has defeated* **producer responsibility laws.** *It's still fighting redemption programs in states that have them. Find out more at bottlebill.org.*

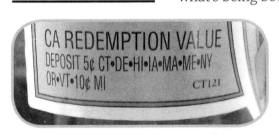

The bigger the corporations, the bigger the impact when they set high standards for their **supply chain** *— the smaller companies providing the supplies they need. If Home Depot demands sustainably grown wood — as it has — lumber companies worldwide have a strong motive to comply.*

No economic or political system is free of problems. Or solutions. Major fixes usually need governments to alter the rules by which economies operate. By granting **subsidies** and **tax breaks,** governments encourage particular industries. For many solutions, confronting vested interests is required — the reason politics is a crucial part of freeing ourselves from our environmental bind.

The profit motive that drives capitalism is like fire: beneficial if controlled, harmful if not. Through politics we can regain that control by rewriting its ground rules. If the result is that energy companies can make more money selling renewables than selling fossil fuels, that's what they'll do. The same profit motive that fueled learning how to process tar sands can be turned to other goals. It all depends on what we demand.

Subsidies *are government payments to businesses to promote production of vital goods.*

Tax breaks *support chosen industries by lowering their expenses for taxes. Fossil-fuel companies receive billions of dollars of such aid and have lobbied successfully against renewables getting the same boost — a major reason wind and solar power lag in the United States.*

Denver (CO) Examiner, 9-19-12

Republican lawmakers attack wind tax credits saying they hurt coal

Because business usually works faster and values innovation more than government, capitalism could speed us toward a safer world rather than being a roadblock. **The Upcycle: Beyond Sustainability—Designing for Abundance** by William McDonough and Michael Braungart gives many examples.

BACKSTORY: OZONE

The crisis that resembled a sci-fi classic

the better to scent you with...

NEW **YARDLEY** SPRAY MIST

in four famous fragrances...

only $2 each (Plus tax)

Can't break, spill, leak or evaporate. The lightest touch scents you instantly, gently, lastingly, with your favorite Yardley fragrance.

The laboratory scene. Scientists discover in 1928 that compounds of carbon, fluorine, and chlorine can help cool, clean, fight fire, and propel aerosol sprays. Chlorofluorocarbons— CFCs—slowly become common in daily life.

But something's not right. Unnoticed, the CFCs rise from cans of shaving cream, deodorants, degreasers, discarded refrigerators, and air conditioners. In 1974, two California chemists theorize that CFCs might reach the stratosphere, react with the ozone there, and turn it into other compounds.

The scream. In 1984 an "ozone hole" is discovered over Antarctica. Ozone is known to absorb cancer-causing UVB rays. Fair-skinned Australians and New Zealanders, already suffering high rates of skin cancers, are alarmed.

It's coming this way! A hole is found over the Northern Hemisphere. Americans quickly ban aerosols, but the hole keeps growing. CFCs released long before are just reaching the ozone.

Showdown. The call goes out worldwide. Delegations meet. In 1987, nations band together against the threat and sign the Montreal Protocol, agreeing to phase out CFCs. The California scientists receive the Nobel Prize.

A dress rehearsal for the climate crisis? The similarities are many:

- An unsuspected side effect of everyday life, building up out of sight over decades

- The need to act on a hypothesis rather than on a certainty

- Opposition from the companies and countries that sold CFCs

- Resistance from developing nations, where refrigeration was just becoming widespread

- Discovery that the problem was growing faster than scientists predicted and would continue long after the causes were addressed

Action was taken based on prudence, without a seeing-is-believing epidemic. Businesses fought the charges against CFCs. They complained about costs and predicted lost jobs but in the end discovered substitutes that turned out to be cheaper. Findings from the atmosphere spurred cooperation among countries. When data worsened, nations sped up the phase-out.

The issue isn't dead. The ozone layer is healthier now but isn't expected to fully recover until late in the century. The substitutes for CFCs still damage ozone to some degree and turn out to be powerful greenhouse gases. The search for alternatives is ongoing. Still, the ozone crisis shows that we can come together to confront problems of global scope before they become outright disasters.

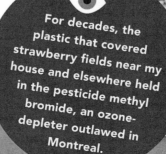

For decades, the plastic that covered strawberry fields near my house and elsewhere held in the pesticide methyl bromide, an ozone-depleter outlawed in Montreal.

Attitudes

science
to the rescue

And why we keep
needing saving

kyping between Toledo and Tahiti. Performing eye surgery with lasers. Carrying ten thousand songs on your MP3 player. Technology's successes are so many and so stunning that there's a default trust that it will solve our environmental problems. And maybe it will.

There's huge appeal there. Changing our gadgets is a breeze compared with changing our behavior. Science can spare leaders from trying to get us to have fewer children, drive less, and cut back on heating and cooling. This is one reason politicians fight for technological fixes, from the Alaska pipeline in the 1970s to carbon capture today. High tech holds out the dream that we can have everything we want: our lifestyle *and* no harmful side effects. Instead of changing our ways, we'll simply change our cars and appliances.

Faith in science is so strong that it can have the same calming effect as denial. Smartphones and social media spread worldwide so quickly that people might assume green breakthroughs can do the same. But eBay and Twitter threatened no titanic vested interests. And

We've been able to double computer memory and speed every two years. Known as Moore's Law, this has held true for half a century.

Business Examiner, 4-25-10

Poll shows most Americans think "green consumerism" enough to avert environmental crisis.

hardware is much tougher to replace than software.

We all hope technology will come through for us. To do so, it will have to avoid two categories of side effects that have dogged it.

It's too effective. "Too much of a good thing" has applied ever since early humans got so good at hunting that they wiped out their prey. The pattern continues.

- Plastic drift nets, bottom trawlers, and sonar are so effective at catching fish that we're quickly driving populations to the point of collapse.

- Chain saws and bulldozers have fast-forwarded deforestation and climate change.

- Nuclear weapons are so lethal that not just the enemy but all humanity is threatened.

"When the bang we make can blow up our world, we have made rather too much progress."

Ronald Wright, *A Short History of Progress*

Solutions become problems.

Technology both solves our problems and causes new ones down the road through unforeseen side effects. Who would have guessed that the synthetic fertilizers that helped prevent famines would lead to depleted oxygen in lakes and river deltas, bringing us fish kills and dead zones? Many substances plaguing us today were yesterday's miracle fixes.

- Lead added to paint increased durability and protection against corrosion.

- Trans fats gave us margarine — cheaper and with a longer shelf life than butter.

- Asbestos was hailed for its fire resistance and insulating properties.

- DDT protected millions from typhus and malaria.

All of the above have since been linked to cancer or other serious health problems and have been restricted or removed at great expense. CFCs joined the roster for their effect on ozone. The latest and greatest addition to the list is fossil fuels.

For a tour of geoengineering and the tinkerers behind it, see Jeff Goodell's book How to Cool the Planet.

↘ Check out the documentary **Waste = Food** for more about the cradle-to-cradle movement.

As the size of problems increases, so do the fixes. Geoengineering ideas to combat global warming, from launching space mirrors to piping deep ocean waters to the surface, have a mad-scientist ring that leads even proponents to worry about future problems.

Testing for side effects isn't always practical. Should we have locked up the printing press for a thousand years while we watched for problems caused by absorbing ink through our fingers? Life is a gamble. We've always been guinea pigs, of necessity; we're simply among the first to realize it.

One way to break the chain of side effects is to exclude them by design. The new field of industrial ecology uses life-cycle analysis to weigh all the ingredients and processes that go into a product. The goal isn't just avoiding hazardous substances during production but leaving waste that's harmless and ready to be reused in new products. This cradle-to-cradle model, replacing cradle-to-grave, is beginning to generate its first products, including shoes made by Puma.

At the same time that faith in science is deep-seated, growing numbers of Americans believe its climate conclusions are a hoax. What's going on? Aside from the impact of the denial campaign, I think you're seeing anti-intellectualism — the belief that the common man knows more than the privileged and well educated. It's this bent that causes our politicians to compete to seem the most folksy, bringing into the White House the heavy twangs of Bill Clinton and George W. Bush. It also supports our right to reject whatever we want to, no matter how many Nobel Prize winners say it's so. Politicians who use common-man skepticism to mock climate worries are drawing on this cultural trait.

Americans are famously practical. We're staunch believers in science when it improves our lives. But when it threatens our beliefs (the theory of evolution) or our financial interests (human-caused climate change), we'll fight it with one hand while accepting its gifts with the other.

"Reality has a well-known liberal bias."

Stephen Colbert, American political satirist, making fun of the "I can believe what I want to" attitude

never **retreat**

Progress as a right

Our dependence on fossil fuels didn't arise from an evil plot but through our curiosity and ingenuity. Coal was seen only as a heat source until we found it could power steam engines. Later we discovered that the gas it gave off when heated could light homes and streets. Gasoline was considered a useless by-product of petroleum — and then came the internal combustion engine.

Necessity is said to be the mother of invention, but the reverse is also true. We tinker and probe, then see if our discovery fills any need, including needs we didn't know we had.

With fossil fuels, new uses multiplied madly until we wove them into every corner of our lives. What used to be luxuries — garage-door openers, dishwashers, cell phones — came to feel like necessities. It's easy to go up the lifestyle ladder but painful climbing down. This is important. It explains another reaction to our predicament: refusing to accept a decline.

An ad from 1981. In the beginning, no one really knew what computers could do besides crunch numbers. Only later did we develop games, then e-mail, then chat rooms, music downloads, online banking, social media, cat videos . . . all things we'd gotten along fine without and weren't sure we needed.

What the heck is Electronic Mail?

Resort compounds from which you never need to leave, like this one in Cancún, Mexico, allow Westerners to keep their lifestyle around them when they travel to developing countries.

> "A man is rich in proportion to the number of things he can afford to let alone."

Henry David Thoreau, American writer. One way to avoid the ladder problem is not to keep going up the rungs. Makers of computers and cell phones have gotten us hooked on the temporary euphoria that comes with new features.

It's not hard to understand. The windfall of cheap fossil fuels that's fueled the West for two centuries got us used to ever-rising living standards. Energy buys convenience. And convenience is addictive — highly so. Each increased dosage quickly becomes our new minimum requirement. You see this whenever gas prices rise and endanger our freedom to drive as much as we want — causing politicians to leap into action on our behalf. They know that whatever level of comfort we're at feels like a must.

Skagit Valley (WA) Herald, 11-27-12

Senators demand Justice Department gas price investigation

To escape from the environmental crunch, we don't need to throw out our entire lifestyle but simply to power it on something other than fossil fuels. We're on the way. Switching to renewables for electricity is probably the easy part. Harder will be getting oil out of transportation and agriculture and the military, as well as all the products it's currently in: the asphalt in your street, the carpet on your floor, the clothes in your closet, and all the plastic around you in furniture, appliances, cars, and packaging. Can we run this film in reverse? Only once have we replaced an energy source so central to our economy and lifestyle: when slave labor was abolished, a change so jarring that its threat brought on war.

When our standard of living is threatened by scarcity and side effects, you'd think we'd cut back. Instead, the common response is to maintain it at any cost. Bluefin tuna is in steep decline, but the tuna-loving Japanese are catching all they can. We know our freshwater aquifers are limited, but we're draining them faster rather than slower. Scarcity was humankind's enemy for so long that resistance to a downshift in lifestyle is strong. At the first international climate summit in 1992, the U.S. delegation's attitude was that America's standard of living wasn't up for negotiation. Every U.S. administration since then has followed the same path.

DASANI.

REMINERALIZED WATER
REVERSE OSMOSIS · NON-CARBONATED

up to 30% plant-based · 100% recyclable bottle

FLUORIDE IONS: 0 ppm
TOTAL DISSOLVED S...

plantbottle

591 mL

Plastics made from corn and other plants are now appearing. Challenges: making them biodegradable or easy to recycle. Though they bypass oil, they require land that's currently given to food.

Jared Diamond's book Collapse *describes societies that kept doing what they'd always done and paid the price. The chapter on Easter Island is typical and compelling.*

Developing countries feel the same. People getting their first paved roads, safe water, electric lights, and refrigerators don't want to march backward any more than the West does.

Using less energy and consuming less — taking a step down the ladder — would make the West's transition to renewables that much easier. What would happen if we cut the amount of stuff we bought in half? We'd save hugely on resources as well as on the energy needed to make them into products. We'd also lose large numbers of jobs. To keep employment up, we need people to keep buying bacon-flavored dental floss and Elvis Presley mouse pads and other nonessentials. The call "Never retreat" comes from us both as consumers and breadwinners.

Poster for Buy Nothing Day, sponsored by the activist group Adbusters

Many have sketched a sustainable economy that doesn't rest on unnecessary consumption. These proposals often favor decentralization — a more dispersed and rural society, with people growing more of their own food and generating more of their own power. This would give us an economy with greater resilience than our current highly connected one.

What's the problem with highly integrated systems? They're efficient and low

cost, but brittle. Ours brings us fruit from
South America and computer parts from China
but leaves us in the lurch if anything inter-
rupts trade. We're so connected that a single
power outage or oil shortage affects millions.
Sicknesses can more easily become epidemics.
The American housing collapse of 2008 quickly
brought on a worldwide recession.

Life used to be much more decentral-
ized. The Transition movement, beginning in
Britain, guides communities toward a lower
energy, more self-sufficient future, with
hundreds of branches active in the United
States and elsewhere. The Slow Food
movement, back-to-the-landers
reviving rural skills, and
those pursuing voluntary
simplicity are pointed in
the same direction.

The Amish aren't the only
ones to reject available
technology. The Arts and
Crafts movement that
began in Britain in the
nineteenth century turned
its back on the Industrial
Revolution and promoted
the handmade over the
mass-produced. You can
see its influence in today's
revival of old skills, from
butchering to brewing to
calligraphy.

What might a major lifestyle downshift feel like? Plenty of recent novels picture frightening futures without Facebook and Krispy Kreme. Real-world Americans experienced a downshift during World War II.

Students can experience Third World life at Heifer International's Global Villages and Global Gateway programs, cooking over fires, sleeping in huts, and dealing with food shortages. More at heifer.org.

The U.S. auto industry stopped making cars and switched to building tanks and planes. Gasoline, milk, meat, coffee, cheese, sugar, heating oil, and shoes were strictly rationed. Could we do it again?

Adaptability is one of humankind's hallmarks. We evolved during difficult climatic times, when temperatures swung between ice ages and warmer interglacial periods, times so challenging that the twenty or so other strains of humans who weren't as flexible all died out. Is that ability to adapt still within us?

Consider a power outage's frustrations, then the gradual adaptation the longer it goes on until dining by lantern light feels almost normal. Use of mass transit goes up when gas prices rise. We adjust to water rationing. When a job is lost in the family, we cut budgets. People think they can't go backward, then find out that they can. We ended up succeeding in getting rid of slavery, after all. Stranger still to a time-traveling slave owner: we no longer even notice its absence.

For more on this topic, see the chapter "A Stormworthy Lineage" in Dianne Dumanoski's book The End of the Long Summer.

**no
limits**

New World,
new
mind-set

I f you've ever flown across the United States, you know: it's so vast and empty that it seems impossible we could ever exhaust its resources. The same goes for Canada and Australia. Geography has left an imprint on these three countries — I'll call them the Big Three — that separates them from the rest of the West. What makes them distinctive?

Extra lucky. Europe was largely deforested, short on fertile land, and prone to famine when Columbus sailed west. The New World he happened upon put an immense deposit of resources into Europe's account — farmland, fish, new crops, forests, metals. The same good luck rescued Americans centuries later when petroleum gushed out of the ground in Pennsylvania just as the flow of whale oil was falling due to overhunting. Huge finds of coal and natural gas followed and continue today, the latest being the Marcellus Shale gas field in the Appalachians and oil finds in North Dakota. Australia is the world's largest coal exporter. The melting of Arctic ice will give Canada and the United States a massive gift of oil, gas, and minerals.

Voyages of discovery may be over but high-tech breakthroughs have taken their

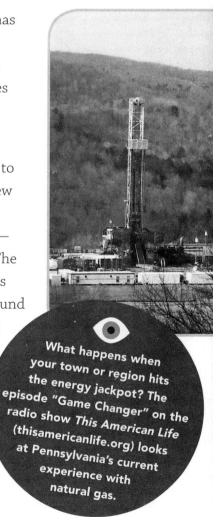

What happens when your town or region hits the energy jackpot? The episode "Game Changer" on the radio show *This American Life* (thisamericanlife.org) looks at Pennsylvania's current experience with natural gas.

place, lifting standards of living without the need of new continents. Silicon Valley's empire rivals the Spanish Empire. All of these have gotten us used to the idea that there's always more around the bend.

Extra large. Five miles of water pipe and power lines in a metropolis might serve 100,000 people but perhaps only one family in the Australian outback. High-density cities are highly efficient. The Big Three are at the other extreme, with their populations spread over huge expanses. The result? Much more steel, concrete, wood, copper wire, and all of infrastructure's other needs per person.

Where population density is low, there aren't enough riders to make public transportation practical to build and operate. This leaves the Big Three dependent on private cars, which use far more energy per person. For such reasons, these countries are always near the top of the list for per capita energy use and carbon footprint, with figures much higher than these of other countries with similar living standards.

Population density per square mile:

Australia: 8

Canada: 9

United States: 85

Europe: 303

Japan: 868

Per capita CO_2 emissions in metric tons in 2009:

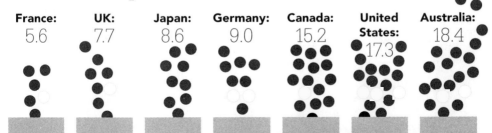

France:	UK:	Japan:	Germany:	Canada:	United States:	Australia:
5.6	7.7	8.6	9.0	15.2	17.3	18.4

Give me more! If you've got six siblings, sharing and hand-me-downs are facts of life. Accepting limited resources comes more naturally to people who've lived in long-settled and crowded conditions. Europe and Japan responded to the 1970s oil shocks by working to both increase supply and reduce demand. The Big Three responded by boosting energy supplies: coal in Australia, tar sands in Canada, and oil in Alaska. This is still the American solution of choice, evidenced by the push to solve freshwater shortages by desalinating seawater and the drive to keep increasing domestic oil production.

On average, European cars are much smaller than American cars.

Conservation is free, available immediately, and large in impact. But it requires recognizing limits, a psychic hurdle for many in these societies. The Big Three are leading the way in researching carbon capture — the fix that would do the least damage to our high-energy consuming lifestyle.

Moving on. With nearly all our ancestors coming from abroad and with families usually moving many times since, changing locale as a solution is in our blood. This combines with our history of windfalls to lead us away from accepting limits. Why settle for less when there's more somewhere else?

Are you living in the country where your parents were born? In the same state? The same city? We're highly mobile, especially on the coasts.

Though our standard of living is among the world's highest, this use-it-up-and-move-on philosophy is the same one found among poor slash-and-burn farmers in the tropics who clear forest, plant crops, and move on when the soil has lost its fertility. Leaving town for new horizons isn't merely the appeal of countless road-trip movies. You can see it in plans for mining expeditions to the asteroid belt and for a new wave of colonization in outer space.

EARTH FIRST!
WE'LL STRIP-MINE THE OTHER PLANETS LATER

This bumper sticker plays on the name of the radical environmental group Earth First!

UPI, 1-26-12

Gingrich: Make the moon the 51st state

Pittsburgh Post-Gazette, 4-27-12

Cosmic Mining— Asteroids Could Yield a Galaxy of Minerals

Omaha Examiner, 1-11-13

Private company seeks applicants to help colonize Mars

Invulnerability. The oceans around the Big Three countries have helped protect them from invasion. The United States watched World Wars I and II as a spectator for years before deciding to enter; Canada and Australia might have done the same had their membership in the British Commonwealth not involved them from the beginning.

Is it that sense of invulnerability that's elevated leaders in all three (at different times) who've scorned climate change worries? Australia and the United States were the only participants in the carbon-curbing 1997 Kyoto talks that didn't ratify the agreement in short order. Canada did, but announced in 2011 that it would withdraw. These three have often sat at their own cafeteria table apart from the rest.

Place matters. But even ingrained attitudes can change. Australia has suffered sci-fi-size droughts, fires, floods, and the rapid dying of its Great Barrier Reef. Ten years after the Kyoto summit, the prime minister who'd opposed that effort was defeated by a candidate who strongly supported it. Geography and history help shape assumptions, but evidence staring us in the face can trump them.

The Great Barrier Reef is the world's largest coral reef. Rising water temperature, increasing acidity, and pollution from agricultural runoff are among the causes of damage.

"All politics is local."

**Tip O'Neill,
American politician**

107

losing
control

A smaller world requires
bigger government

S mokers used to light up every-where, from airplane seats to doctors' waiting rooms. No one knew that secondhand smoke was causing the same diseases as firsthand smoke — and then the news came. Suddenly, smoking went from a private act with no limits except age to an activity that was regulated for the public's health. First came nonsmoking sections in restaurants and airplanes, then outright bans.

As we keep discovering the harmful effects of what we're putting into the environment, the public sphere keeps growing. Managing it is the job of government. We create laws and courts to have a way to solve conflicts in the public realm. But not everyone is happy.

Individuals. Living in groups brings us benefits galore, from public libraries to take-out pizza, but we give up lots of individual rights in the bargain. Your loud party has to get quiet at 10 p.m. You can't build a house without complying with building codes or keep horses in your tiny urban backyard. This is a bargain we sometimes regret. Literature lives off the clash between individual desires and society's demands: Romeo and Juliet defying their families, Huck Finn breaking slavery's codes, Katniss battling her government.

The Libertarian Party in the United States has built a political movement around <u>small government</u> that opposes taxes, zoning laws, business regulation, and other checks on our freedom. You can read its positions at **lp.org.**

Defense of individual rights, from the right to own guns to opposition to taxes, is so fierce in the United States that politicians themselves have been leading the charge against government. Environmentalists, with their impact reports, zoning laws, and love of inconspicuous endangered species, are frequent targets of anger.

Business. Rachel Carson's 1962 book *Silent Spring* was the first shot in the war to force corporations to address their effects on the environment. Since taking this responsibility costs them money, many have spent decades at war against the Clean Air Act, the Clean Water Act, and the EPA.

Regulations try to protect our health and the planet's. Read the editorials in the *Wall Street Journal,* and you'll see the business world's view of them — burdensome, unneeded, and harmful. Seat belts, turn signals, unleaded gas, antipollution devices,

"If the U.S. Environmental Protection Agency does not suspend the catalytic converter rule, it will cause Ford to shut down and would result in: **(1)** reduction in gross national product by $17 billion; **(2)** increased unemployment of 800,000; and **(3)** decreased tax receipts of $5 billion at all levels of government so that some local governments would become insolvent."

Ford president Lee Iacocca, 1973. None of his predictions came to pass when pollution-cutting catalytic converters became mandatory.

airbags, higher gas mileage — all were fought
hard by the U.S. auto industry until government forced their adoption.

Instead of added costs bringing ruin, new
challenges have often spurred technological
growth spurts and cost-saving efficiencies.
As more of the world market demands safe
goods that are safely produced, some companies have started moving this way without
being coerced. Others spend millions instead
on lobbying against regulations, pressing their
case through politicians who warn of lost jobs
and higher prices, sidestepping the environmental problems at the root.

Odessa (TX) American, 10-18-11

Perry calls EPA a job killer
— Texas governor slashed
environmental enforcement

Nations. Factories and power plants in southern China have caused a cloud of pollution known as the "Asian brown cloud" over India and Pakistan. Whale populations worldwide are endangered, but Japan, Norway, and Iceland have continued whaling in spite of a ban. In these cases, the players are nations. Who's going to tell them what to do? Sometimes the countries involved create their own governing group, like the eighty-nine-member International Whaling Commission. With climate change and many other issues, it falls to the United Nations (U.N.).

The tragedy of the commons *is a term for the economic pressure to overexploit a shared resource, like fish or grazing land, until it's destroyed. The logic: even though future generations will suffer, if everyone's doing it, I might as well do it, too.*

The U.N.'s challenges are many. Reaching a decision with a group so large and diverse is tough. Since the U.N. lacks the power that a nation has over its people, enforcement is difficult. It's supported by dues from member nations, who might let payments slide or withhold them in protest. Most important, nations see themselves as <u>sovereign</u> — independent of outside control — and resent any check on their behavior. Though the United States spearheaded the U.N.'s creation after World War II in hopes of preventing future world wars, some Americans feel threatened by world government no matter how frail.

Individuals, businesses, and nations share the same objection: governments restrict us, stifling our narrow interests so as to protect broader ones. The quarrel between those interests is loud, especially in the United States where individual freedom stands atop the pyramid of values. Tune in to many talk radio shows and you'll hear hosts as well as callers lash out at anyone who'd curb our wishes. This regression smacks of childhood, but politicians have given it legitimacy.

Where government is weak, individuals will sometimes rush in to protect the public sphere. You can see them take on a utility company in the movie *Erin Brockovich* and the Japanese whaling fleet in the TV show *Whale Wars*.

It's tough to solve environmental issues — public-sphere problems requiring government — when government is seen by many as a villain. It's interesting to watch what happens when weather and financial disasters strike: everyone wants government help, from flooded-out farmers to bankers who've spent a lifetime bashing Washington. How to explain such inconsistency? Just as with science, we support government when it benefits us but reject it when it doesn't.

Cognitive dissonance *is the mental tension created by holding two conflicting opinions. This is often solved through* **rationalization:** *coming up with justifications for our acts or beliefs. We expect beliefs and actions to be consistent;* **hypocrisy** *is the charge leveled at violators.*

BACKSTORY: KYOTO

The world tries to come to grips with greenhouse gases

Alarming measurements, a concerned public, international action . . .
The greenhouse-gas crisis followed ozone's path, then swerved sharply.
What happened?

Rio de Janeiro, 1992. The first United Nations summit to tackle climate change settled only on general goals. The West recognized that it had released most of the greenhouse gases and agreed to lower its emissions. The developing world, in the midst of modernizing, wouldn't follow suit yet, but would work toward a low-carbon future with the help of money and technology from the West. The agreed-upon target: returning to 1990's level of emissions in 2000. This was voluntary. Would you clean your room if you didn't really have to? Countries are no different. Climate news worsened, emissions kept rising, and pressure built for a binding treaty—the reason for the subsequent summit in Kyoto, Japan.

Kyoto, 1997. Time for the hard part: specifying cuts that would be binding rather than voluntary. The West as a whole agreed to reduce its emissions to 5 percent below 1990 levels by 2012, with Europe cutting back 8 percent, the United States 7 percent, and Canada and Japan 6 percent. Russia was allowed to keep its current level, while Australia was allowed to *increase* its output by 8 percent. There was no target for non-Western countries.

The treaty, known as the Kyoto Protocol, had to be approved by nations at home. Virtually every country did so except Australia and the United States. Months before the Kyoto talks took place, carmakers and labor and fossil-fuel interests lobbied American politicians. Claiming the economic cost would be too great, the Senate passed a resolution opposing approval of any treaty that exempted developing countries. Without American participation, the West's 5 percent cut shrank to 2 percent.

After Kyoto. Few nations have been willing to risk their economies or lifestyles for the sake of climate. Instead of the long view, the short one has dominated; instead of the global view, countries are still looking out for themselves.

• The United States has refused to make cuts until China (the top greenhouse-gas emitter) and India do the same, turning its back on the West's original offer to cut first. The recession that began in 2008 pressed U.S. politicians to restart the economy and bump up emissions rather than cut them. It also shelved Western promises of money and technology.

Anti-Kyoto protestors in Washington

Low-lying islands are pleading for action. Here, the cabinet of the Maldive Islands, in the Indian Ocean, meets underwater to publicize rising sea levels.

- China and India felt betrayed by the U.S. withdrawal and are no more excited about the bitter pill of carbon cuts than the West is. With so much fat to trim in the West's carbon diet, they argue, shouldn't cuts take place there rather than in countries just getting paved roads and refrigerated meat?

- Europe suffered more than 70,000 deaths in the heat wave of 2003. Governments in Europe, Japan, and Australia have often supported stricter standards and have shown the will to impose them on business and the public.

- The poorest nations want stronger measures, too. Innocent bystanders on the global stage, they've done the least to cause the problem but will likely suffer most since their weaker governments are less able to cope with food, weather, and refugee problems.

Blame, pleas, secret alliances, and empty claims of success have characterized the yearly summits, with the United States and China working together to block progress. This has irked the countries that are tackling their targets. The United Kingdom's 2008 Climate Change Act pledged to cut emissions an astounding 80 percent below 1990 levels by 2050—the first country to commit itself to such major cuts. Australia and Japan have launched similar efforts. Many American cities have set their own carbon-cutting goals in the absence of leadership in Washington.

⤴ To see if your city is among them, check **http://www.gcp-urcm.org/Resources/CityActionPlans#Namerica.**

There's a widely recognized need to build a replacement for the Kyoto Protocol that includes China, India, and the United States.

Reducing greenhouse gases turns out to be far harder than dealing with CFCs. It asks much more of science, our economies, our politicians, and the public—so much that only a few countries have been willing to dive in. CO_2 in the atmosphere was at 365 ppm during the Kyoto meetings; instead of going down, it's now up to 400 ppm. Will nations in the next decade begin asking more of themselves?

Eyes Abroad
and Ahead

conflict

Environmental stress brings political strife

Global warming is melting the Arctic's thin layer of ice, bringing closer the possibility of year-round drilling for a vast trove of oil and gas. Even nations with no Arctic real estate, like China, are jockeying for position to get a share.

We find a plentiful food source. Our numbers grow until there's no longer enough food. We go looking for more fish or more game or more land. If the new source is already claimed, we fight or trade for it. If we get it, our numbers go up again.

This has been the pattern since our spear-throwing days. Rome was once a mere village whose search for food and secure borders stretched it into an empire. This expansion required constant warfare, transforming Mars, a god of crops, into Rome's god of war.

Needs other than food can bring conflict and colonization. Ancient Egypt occupied Syria to get timber for its armies' chariots. Britain colonized North America in part to get wood for its navy's ships after cutting down its own forests.

Today, the key hunt is for energy. Fuel might as well be food, as factories, transportation, and agriculture can't exist without it. Metals, water, and food are vital as well. Consumption levels have risen so high that all countries — even those with the most resources — have to look beyond their borders. Those levels have skyrocketed outside of the West. Suddenly, Indonesia and

Malaysia and China and India are competing with the United States and western Europe, all desperately searching for new supplies. Scarcity brings competition, conflict, and innovation, and lies behind many of the world's headlines.

Oil and gas. Fossil fuels are so vital that countries that have more than they need—think the Middle East—suddenly cast huge shadows on the world stage. Mighty superpowers are reduced to begging. Weapons are their most popular offering. China armed Sudan to get its oil in return; the United States did the same with Saudi Arabia. Buyers promise military alliances, diplomatic aid, and the know-how and infrastructure to get the fuel. They might try an economic invasion, like China's attempt to buy the American company Unocal and its fossil-fuel holdings. Or they might go to war.

- The growth of American suburbs and car dependence caused oil demand to rise far beyond domestic supplies. The United States waged two recent wars that helped ensure its access to oil: fighting Iraq for control of oil-rich Kuwait in the Gulf War, then occupying Iraq during the Iraq War. The United States is determined never to face shortages from another oil embargo, a motive for the drilling technology that's provided new finds and the reason for our increasing dependence on more reliable supplies from Canada.

- The Caspian Sea region is the site of a scramble among Iran, Russia, the United States, and many other countries for gigantic finds of oil and natural gas, with disputes over borders, rights, and the building of pipelines.

Iraqis inspect the palace of former leader Saddam Hussein. Lots of resources aren't always a good thing. Such jackpots have often led to corruption, poor economic growth, and wider gaps between rulers and their people—the meaning behind the term the resource curse.

- Underwater fossil fuel finds have led to conflict between China and its neighbors on the South China Sea, between Turkey and Greece, and between Argentina and Britain.

- The Arctic is another battleground, with a large cast of competitors fighting over oil and gas as well as vital rare earth elements used in everything from cell phones to solar panels.

Food. Hunger fanned the twentieth-century revolutions in Russia, China, and Mexico. It's still driving headlines. The jump in meat eating, the spread of biofuel crops, and losses from climate change have undercut harvests as well as political stability. It's no accident that the world's most politically volatile countries — Somalia, Iraq, Haiti, Pakistan — feature overpopulation and over-stressed environments. Hungry, unemployed men have little to lose in taking up arms.

Food riot in Tunisia in 2011

- Food shortages and high prices played a role in the revolts that began in 2010 in Tunisia and swept through Egypt, Yemen, Libya, and Syria.

- Rwanda possessed exhausted land, stripped forests, and Africa's densest population attempting to survive on ever-smaller and steeper plots. These conditions helped lead to the genocide of 800,000 people in 1994.

- Competition for land between herdsmen and farmers was the cause of thousands of deaths in 2003–2008 in Sudan's Darfur region. The same tensions have exploded in Nigeria. A conflict that seems to be religious and cultural — such as Nigeria's Muslim herdsmen versus Christian farmers — often has roots in reduced **carrying capacity.**

Carrying capacity *is an area's ability to support its population.*

Water. Rivers often pass through several countries, leaving downstream users fearful of losing water to upstream neighbors. Arab nations' plan to divert the Jordan River to deprive Israel of water helped spark the 1967 Six-Day War. Competition for shared river and lake resources pits China against India, India against Bangladesh, Egypt against Ethiopia, the United States against Mexico, Georgia against Alabama, and northern California against southern California.

Birmingham (AL) News, 8-28-11

Feeding Atlanta at Alabama's expense, Georgia fights to keep Lake Lanier water for itself

Refugees. Some groups crossing borders have no guns. These are the climate refugees, pushed by spreading deserts and lengthening drought in Africa, Brazil, China, India, Iran, Central America, and other regions. This exodus is already in progress. Some move to other parts of their countries; others try to get to the wealthier West.

Sydney (Australia) Morning Herald, 1-7-12

Climate Change Castaways Consider Move to Australia

Treatment of illegal immigrants in the United States will give you an idea of how welcome refugees are. They mean more mouths to feed, more health-care needs, and emergency housing issues, often in countries struggling to take care of their own — a category even affluent nations feel they fall into. Everyone's happy at Halloween, with candy flowing from every door; plenty brings peace. Scarcity brings strife. Your three cousins will be moving into your bedroom with you — indefinitely?

We've been here before. The United States had its own wave of climate refugees in the 1930s — the Dust Bowl migrants who fled Texas, Oklahoma, and surrounding states. Drought and overcultivation of marginal lands caused topsoil to blow away and led more than two million people to leave their homes. Not all were welcomed. Los Angeles sent a "bum brigade" of policemen to try to turn them back at the California border.

Along with those desperate for water are the many who'll be fleeing it if sea-level rise continues. This could push many millions from their homes in China, India, Bangladesh, Nigeria, Egypt, and the Gulf and Atlantic coasts of the United States — a recipe for conflict on a massive scale.

For more, see the 2010 documentary *Climate Refugees.*

If environmental stress can lead to competition and discord, the opposite is also true. Building up soil, protecting forests and fish stocks, and avoiding overpopulation and climate change all work to prevent conflict before it starts. Good stewardship might not seem to be doing anything. What's not visible is the savings in lives and livelihoods and the expense and trauma of wars never declared, mass migrations never made, and disasters that never had to be cleaned up.

chindia

Why your future is tied to China and India

Your backpack says "Made in China." Your computer's customer-service number ends up taking you to India. But your most important links to these countries might be their effect on the ecosystem we all share. Together they hold a third of the world's people, vastly multiplying the impact of their every twitch. The United States, Canada, and Australia are large, but these two seem to own the word *largest*.

To cut costs, offshoring has moved many American jobs to countries where labor is cheaper. Pollution is offshored by having our products manufactured abroad and later shipped again to be disassembled by workers like this man in India.

When China filled the reservoir behind its Three Gorges Dam—the world's largest—the water's weight was so great that it caused a wobble in the Earth's rotation.

People. China has the world's largest population — 1.3 billion people, four times the number in the United States. Though urbanization and its 1979 one-child policy has slowed growth dramatically, China is still growing and has more than one hundred cities of one million or more.

India is struggling to lower its growth rate, hampered by varying policies in its twenty-eight states and past scandals over steriliza-tions and vasectomies. Its higher rate puts it on track to pass China by 2050. In both countries, population is rushing toward the cities, leading Asia to regain the dominance it enjoyed until the Industrial Revolution.

The world's three most populous cities in 1500, 1950, and 2000:

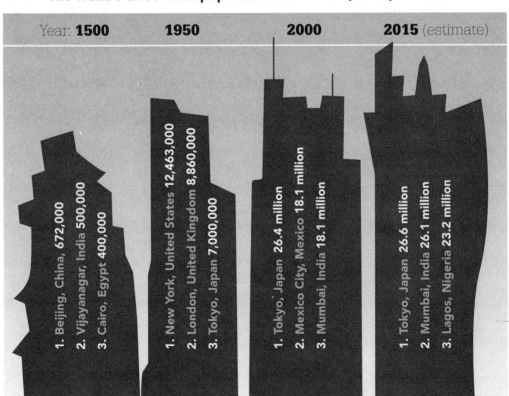

Year: **1500** **1950** **2000** **2015** (estimate)

1. Beijing, China, 672,000
2. Vijayanagar, India 500,000
3. Cairo, Egypt 400,000

1. New York, United States 12,463,000
2. London, United Kingdom 8,860,000
3. Tokyo, Japan 7,000,000

1. Tokyo, Japan 26.4 million
2. Mexico City, Mexico 18.1 million
3. Mumbai, India 18.1 million

1. Tokyo, Japan 26.6 million
2. Mumbai, India 26.1 million
3. Lagos, Nigeria 23.2 million

Economy. Mix this influx of workers with the imported Western industrial system, add in the demand that these new consumers create, factor in major government spending on infrastructure, and you have exploding economies that are quickly lifting standards of living. China is weighted toward manufacturing, India toward services — information technology, engineering, medicine.

With prosperity rising, both countries are buying more and more of the goods and services that they used to export. The U.S. economy, the world's largest for a century, is expected to be passed by China's in short order, with India a few decades behind.

Resources. Like the West a century ago, China and India are feverishly building, laying roads, and electrifying. This push has caused their demand for energy to soar and is driving massive worldwide mining of copper, iron, aluminum, and other metals. The pressure on their renewable resources — soil, water, forests — has been extra-large as well. With rivers drying up in the more populous north, China has begun immense canal projects to divert water from its rivers in the south, alarming India over possible water losses.

Edward Burtynsky has built a career on photographing the mines, factories, and industrial zones that lie behind our products. Check out his book **Manufactured Landscapes: The Photographs of Edward Burtynsky**—focused on China—or his talk at **ted.com.**

131

Consumption.

Cell phones, refrigerators, and air-conditioning, all rare until recently, are increasingly common. The coming of cars dwarfs them all in import. The materials to build them, the gasoline to run them, the highways and gas stations and parking lots to support them, the sprawl they foster, and the emissions they release all combine to transform a country's environmental profile when they take hold. China is predicted to top the United States in car sales by 2020, despite traffic jams so fearsome that they can last days. Cars' convenience is both toxic and intoxicating, as Americans know well.

India's low-priced, two-cylinder Tata Nano was released in 2009 as a car for the masses. Predictions that it would put the entire country on four wheels proved false, due in part to a few of the cars catching fire, but other cars are selling well.

Energy.

Both China and India depend heavily on coal for electricity. Despite huge resources, their mines can't keep up with demand, and both countries must now scour the world for supplies to import. Coal's side effects are pushing major investment in solar, wind, nuclear, and dams; the Three Gorges Dam and others make China the world leader in hydropower. Since both nations are still building their energy systems, they have the chance to partially leapfrog the West and go directly to clean power for a growing slice of their energy. Their top priority, however, is present demand and feeding their fast-growing economies.

Because coal is plentiful and cheap, both will keep burning it despite its downsides.

Pollution. These big economies come with big side effects. The same factories bringing prosperity to China have produced "cancer villages" from polluted drinking water. The boom in refrigeration in both China and India is causing new damage to the ozone layer since some of today's coolants are only slightly less harmful than the CFCs they replaced. Soil erosion, water and air pollution, and deforestation—boosted in China by demand for disposable chopsticks—are major problems.

China recently passed the United States for the honor of being the world's largest emitter of greenhouse gases. India is currently number three. Climate-related problems abound, from the melting of Himalayan glaciers vital to India's water supply to the rolling deserts in China's northwest to crop losses and refugees from both droughts and floods.

New York Times, 2-1-12

India's Air the World's Unhealthiest, Study Says

Action. With that list, it's no surprise that global warming is taken seriously in China and India. With every new economic milestone, these nations' effect on climate mounts. What are their governments doing to change course?

India has placed a **carbon tax** on coal — the first country in Asia to do so — and is planning a **cap and trade** program for its largest greenhouse-gas emitters. China is building coal-fired plants at a frenetic pace but is also leading the way in more efficient, less polluting designs. It's shifted millions of riders of gas-powered scooters to electric bikes. Preparing for the age of renewables, it's given huge subsidies to its companies building solar panels and wind turbines, allowing prices so low that other countries' industries can't compete.

A **carbon tax** *is one added to fossil fuels, usually helping fund research in alternatives.*

Cap and trade *programs allow major emitters like power plants and steel mills a baseline emission — their cap. To emit more, companies have to buy credits from those who emit less. Both tactics give a financial advantage to those who emit fewer greenhouse gases.*

"If we do not change our direction, we are likely to end up where we are going."

Chinese proverb

The Great Wall was meant to hold back nomadic invaders. The "Green Wall of China" is a series of strips of forest planned to extend nearly 3,000 miles by 2050. Its purpose is to hold down soil and hold back China's latest invader—the spreading Gobi Desert.

Numbers and lifestyle are key here, as elsewhere. The lifestyle of the average Indian produces roughly one-twentieth the amount of greenhouse gases as that of the average American, but India's population is so large that the two countries emit similar amounts. This puts China and India in a bind. The Earth and its climate couldn't bear the weight of those huge populations living the West's lifestyle. But once you start up the development ladder, no one wants to go backward. Will China and India be able to ground their standard of living on green power and fewer resources and keep their footprints to a manageable size?

What's it like to live in India or China? **Expat-blog.com** offers blogs by Westerners working, studying, or traveling there as well as in other countries.

135

fixes

What works, what doesn't

Floating wind farms, fuel from algae, painting roofs white to reflect sunlight, raising meat in labs without animals. . . . For every environmental problem, we've come up with scores of answers. Only time will separate the hits from the misses. In the meantime, what about the bigger picture on solutions?

Morale. It's easy to feel overwhelmed. Lists of downward-spiraling systems that don't mention how we can help leave us feeling paralyzed and hopeless. Remember, though, that no one foresaw the statues of Lenin coming down and the mighty Soviet Union suddenly vanishing — until it happened. The same goes for apartheid in South Africa and segregation in the American South. We're capable of big changes, sometimes big, swift changes. Just ask Louis XVI of France.

Private fixes. Changes in your personal sphere — what you buy, how you get around — have the great advantage that they're in your power to make right now, without getting a bill through Congress. It feels good to have your actions aligned with your beliefs. The downside is that the impact is small. Then again, small acts multiplied by thousands fueled the movements that gave women the vote, ended segregation, and created our first environmental protections. Our individual actions change the microclimate around us. Anywhere you start is useful.

⇗ Paul Hawken's book ***Blessed Unrest: How the Largest Movement in the World Came into Being, and Why No One Saw It Coming*** estimates there are one million different groups working around the world on environmental and social issues. You can browse and search at **wiser.org**.

Public fixes. Changing policies and leaders instead of light bulbs offers a bigger payoff but is harder to accomplish. This is usually a job for a group. Name a need and some organization is probably working on it. Possible challenges: personality conflicts, impatience with lack of progress, the agony of defeat. Probable benefits: camaraderie, learning curves, performing on the big stage.

Shadow solutions. Eating locally grown foods saves on transportation, but how crops are grown — irrigation, pesticides, fertilizers — turns out to be a more important gauge of their carbon footprint. Recycling reduces mining and energy use, but its difficulties and energy needs make it a modest help rather than a cure-all. Carpool lanes seem a good thing, but making driving easier perpetuates car use. Some common-sense fixes turn out to be suspect. From **carbon offsets** to products with green labels, read the fine print on solutions.

Most recycling is **downcycling** — *converting waste into materials of lesser quality. Office paper might become cardboard, then toilet paper, then its wood fibers leave the system.* **Upcycling** *creates materials or products of higher quality; see hipcycle.com for bookends made from 45 rpm records and much more.*

Carbon offsets — *also called* **carbon credits** — *are donations to programs that work to reduce greenhouse gases (through reforestation, mass transit, and other means) so as to shrink the footprint of high-CO_2 activities. If the greenhouse gases added to the atmosphere are balanced by offsets, the activity is* **carbon neutral** — *a status many schools, businesses, and cities are working toward. Because of fraud — many sellers of offsets never perform the promised services — offsets are considered risky. Do your research.*

Changing behavior. Asking people to drive less doesn't work, but miles fall whenever gas prices shoot up. Attitudes haven't changed — we still love driving's convenience — but our behavior has. The moral: actions change quickly when we're compelled.

This is good news. Sometimes nature does the compelling. Sometimes the economy or government does, through oil shortages or tobacco taxes or water rationing. We grumble but change. It's all about setting up the rules that will get the results you want. The current rules have given us our current fix. Since government sets the rules — who gets tax breaks, what safety regulations are enforced, what gas-mileage standards automakers need to meet — political pushing will be required. Alter the rules and huge changes can result.

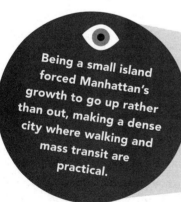

Being a small island forced Manhattan's growth to go up rather than out, making a dense city where walking and mass transit are practical.

coming soon

What to watch for

I t's a dramatic moment in history. You have a front-row seat. What might lie ahead?

Forecasting the environment is tough. Over and over, pessimistic predictions that fossil fuels were running out have been made obsolete by new finds and new methods. Many climate predictions, by contrast, have been too optimistic: worrisome figures have usually outstripped projections.

Amid all the predictions, you'll probably hear voices around you crying, "All is lost." Some say it from belief in an apocalypse predicted in the Bible and may even welcome environmental collapse as confirmation of the Bible's truth. Nonreligious people may say it from the assumption that humanity deserves to be punished for its environmental sins. Both types are confusing what they believe *ought* to be with what *will* be — a prescription for poor forecasting. You'll hear others moan it out of apathy, exempting themselves from the need

Horizontal drilling and fracking have caused an energy boom in North Dakota. See "America Strikes New Oil" in the March 2013 *National Geographic* for a look at what's happening.

to do anything, the seductive bliss offered by regression.

What's beyond doubt is that the topics below will keep generating headlines around you and drive changes rolling across your region and down your block. How to keep on top of what's happening? Hometown newspapers and TV stations are tightly focused on local news and might not offer much on the environment. For the bigger picture, try a bigger newspaper's website. Separate sections for the environment are rare; try science, health, or technology. See what you think of climatedesk.org, enn.com, grist.org, insideclimatenews.org, and the Ecocentric page on *Time* magazine's website. Take the salad bar approach: pick from lots of sources.

For real-time estimated figures on population, consumption, energy, and food, check out **worldometers.info.**

THE NEAR FUTURE

Fracking fights.

The huge new natural gas fields that fracking can exploit would give the U.S. more much energy independence and help turn the country away from coal. Arguing against it are side effects, from carcinogens in groundwater to earthquakes when wastewater is disposed

of underground. Supporters on both sides are ready for battle. Given drilling interests' coziness with politicians, fracking seems likely to spread far, wide, and fast unless it causes a PR disaster in the manner of Three Mile Island.

The Three Mile Island nuclear power plant near Harrisburg, Pennsylvania, suffered a partial meltdown in 1979. The uncertainty and fear led thousands to evacuate and shook Americans' faith in nuclear power.

Power shifts.

The pressure is on coal — from the public and from cheap natural gas. If your electricity comes from coal, your power plant may close, convert to burning natural gas, or switch to biomass — wood pellets or other plant material. That same cheap gas is undercutting wind and solar as well. In green energy's favor: many states are now requiring that their **energy portfolio** contain renewables. Because of government support, scale, and the absence of cost for carbon pollution, fossil fuels have always been cheaper than renewables. When those factors change, look for major power shifts. In Australia, it's now cheaper to get electricity from wind than from coal or gas.

An **energy portfolio** *is the mix of power sources drawn on for energy. A typical* **portfolio standard** *might require a state to get 25 percent of its electricity from renewables by 2025 — the case in Ohio. More than half of U.S. states have such standards. Is yours among them? Keep tabs on your statehouse, where forces pro and con fight over bills to set these standards, usually out of the public's sight.*

The divestment campaign.

Ever wonder where the scholarship money you'll be applying for comes from? It comes from endowments — donations that are put into stocks and other investments to increase their value. Environmental groups have found a new lever in the drive to lower greenhouse gases: pressuring universities to divest their endowment funds of all fossil-fuel stocks. This push is quite likely coming to a college near you. The same drive is taking place with funds managed by churches and by cities and states that make pension payments to retirees.

Vassar College Fossil Fuel Divestment Campaign page on Facebook

Climate summits.

Pressure is building on the United States, China, and India. They'll likely be forced to start cutting greenhouse gases; the question is how much. With lifestyle and jobs at stake, reductions big enough to matter seem unlikely unless nature hits back at those countries even more force-fully than at present. So far, the only major decline in greenhouse gases has come unin-tentionally — from the drop in production, building, driving, and shopping caused by the 2008 recession.

> "History teaches us that men and nations behave wisely once they have exhausted all other alternatives."
>
> **Abba Eban, Israeli diplomat**

Preparedness. The Dutch are relocating some residents to higher ground. Peru is experimenting with painting mountain peaks white to reflect heat and slow the melting of its glaciers. Though little support has come from Washington, climate task forces aiming at cutting carbon and preparing for climate change have sprouted up in American cities, counties, states, universities, and school districts. Chances are there's one, or one coming, near you.

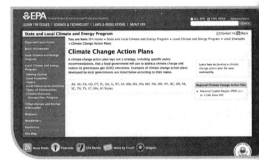

FURTHER OUT

Taxing carbon. Cap and trade and carbon taxes are already in place in many countries. California's cap and trade program, the first in the United States, is just getting under way. By making dirty energy more expensive, both methods use the market to stimulate greener power. American fossil-fuel companies fought both proposals for decades, then realized that getting more heavily into natural gas would let them make money selling credits to companies burning coal. If howls from the weather and from climate summits get loud enough, the U.S. federal government might finally get on board.

Electric cars. The first gas-electric hybrids were too expensive up front for many Americans. Will the next generation and

The EPA maintains a roster of climate-change action plans—indexed by state, summarizing the plan's goals, and giving its website—at **http://www.epa.gov /statelocalclimate /local/local-examples /action-plans.html.**

all-electric plug-ins win over more drivers? Range and the need for charging stations are hurdles. Most all-electric cars still burn fossil fuels, since that's how two-thirds of U.S. electricity is made, but as the grid gets cleaner, so will the cars.

Check out Mason Inman's "The True Cost of Fossil Fuels" in the April 2013 *Scientific American* to see how much more efficient it is to power a car with electricity (even from coal) than it is to run it on oil.

Carbon capture. Expect a major effort here, in the field and with public opinion, pushed by the coal lobby. Success would let them wring more profit from their investment before coal's era closes. The added cost of carbon capture and storage is so great, however, that it might be impractical, especially if coal is competing against cheap natural gas. Most environmentalists see CCS research as encouraging coal burning and will likely battle to put the money toward clean energy instead. Unsafe as coal is, its abundance will keep it being burned worldwide. Consider this argument: teenagers will have sex, so they better have condoms; countries will burn coal, so we better have carbon capture.

Cities and suburbs. Downtowns were long thought the most desirable places to live. Suburbs changed all that. Now we've rediscovered the benefits of living close to work and being able to walk to the store. Watch for a flow back to city centers, especially by the young, and a rethinking of suburbs.

Carrying capacity. The rate of population growth may be slowing, but will the Earth's carrying capacity fall even more steeply due to climate's effect on harvests? Look for GMO crops resistant to floods and higher temperatures to be used ever more widely, to keep us ahead of Malthus's prediction.

Geoengineering. Procrastinators know it well: the less time you have, the fewer choices you've got and the more desperate your actions. If CO_2 levels haven't stopped growing, geoengineering will increasingly look like our best hope. Watch for the buildup.

Miracle fuels. Hydrogen for transportation? Nuclear fusion for electricity? Something not yet imagined? One of these could be a game-changer in the quest to replace fossil fuels. The miracle needed isn't just abundant, clean power but also something that can be put into place quickly. A search for "fuel" at ted.com will bring you a choice of videos by miracle-fuel proponents.

For more on the shift to city living, see Alan Ehrenhalt's book *The Great Inversion* or the interview with him at **smartplanet.com.** And check out Ellen Dunham-Jones's TED talk about retrofitting suburbia.

NPR, 5-29-10

Geoengineering: "A Bad Idea Whose Time Has Come"

Texas wildfire, 2011. The United States is beginning to feel extreme weather close-up, with eight climate-related disasters in 2011 that each did more than $1 billion in damage, including the extensive wildfires in Texas; 2012 brought eleven such events.

ATTITUDE CHANGES

Reacting and preparing.

The gist of normalcy bias is that we're reluctant to prepare for disasters we've never experienced. The flip side is that we're willing to do so for disasters we've known. Hurricane Sandy showed the most densely populated portion of the United States what extreme weather is like and what rising waters can do. Further extra-large weather events could shock us into the kind of action that we haven't been able to demand of ourselves. Europeans and Australians are ahead of the United States in large part because of the devastating fires, floods, and heat waves they've suffered. We knew Germany and Japan had been overrunning other countries in World War II, but it took the attack on Pearl Harbor to impel us to act. The same could happen again.

Vested interests. Would vested interests actually drag the world to its doom rather than lose profits? It sounds crazy, but ruling groups are usually too invested in the system that gives them money and power to want to change it. Many have preferred steering the same course even if it leads to disaster, from the nobility overthrown by the Russian revolution to the Detroit CEOs whose loyalty to shoddy gas-guzzlers led their companies to disaster. Political upheavals sometimes remove them from power. Droughts, deforestation, and sapped soils and economies have brought a slower death to their societies.

For a chronicle of political and military blindness through the ages, check out Barbara Tuchman's top-notch book The March of Folly: From Troy to Vietnam.

Anger over the vast wealth, power, and perks enjoyed by the few at the top of American society fueled 2011's Occupy Wall Street movement, which began in New York City and spread worldwide.

THE 99% ARE
100% FED U

A look at fossil-fuel companies' websites might convince you they've changed. But behind the greenwashing, they're investing billions in future drilling in the Arctic, Africa, Asia, and the United States. That's what they do, and there's so much oil and gas to be had and so many customers that there's no incentive to alter course. This trend could change if governments pressured by citizens pressured by weather demand a new course. Watch then for these companies to pay more than lip service to renewables; they'll want to stay on top of the post-carbon world as well.

Revising views. Friends of the environment likely have a variety of attitude adjustments of their own coming. Nuclear power has been embraced by some who fought it for decades, as the full price of fossil fuels has become known. DDT poisoned ecosystems, but banning it led to millions of deaths from malaria; the World Wildlife Fund now supports its limited use. Many greens are now singing the praises of city living. Others may decide that they need to make friends with GMOs and even gambling with geoengineering.

You can see the change in thinking in the subtitle of early environmentalist Stewart Brand's recent book:

WHOLE EARTH DISCIPLINE
WHY DENSE CITIES, NUCLEAR POWER, TRANSGENIC CROPS, RESTORED WILDLANDS, AND GEOENGINEERING ARE NECESSARY.
STEWART BRAND

Thinking globally. Hurricane Sandy proved that we pay attention to what's near. That should be an argument against global thinking. But as the consequences of the environmental crunch are felt in ever more places, people all over the world are finding themselves on the front lines of the same conflict. You may see the dawning of a global perspective that couldn't have emerged until this point.

One community. This global view can't help but be furthered by the computer and cell phone, which have connected the planet's people in ways unthinkable just a few years ago. Three-quarters of the world now uses cell phones, the vast majority in developing countries, which found cell phone infrastructure far cheaper and faster to build than landlines.

One-third of the world is now connected to the Internet and its one trillion web pages. For what this means, check out Clay Shirky's TED talk, "How Social Media Can Make History," and the chapter "The Global Mind" in Al Gore's book The Future.

The effect has been startling. Who could have predicted that texting and cell phone cameras would help bring down dictators across the Middle East? From solving problems through crowdsourcing to raising funds through crowd funding, from online citizen science projects to medical videos that overcome distance and language barriers, these tools have fostered a new sense of community that ignores borders. The computer has been vital in analyzing data and predicting outcomes. Its ability to link us together may prove just as valuable. It couldn't have come at a better time.

A nurse in Nepal shows a new mother one of Global Health Media Project's cell phone videos on newborn health.

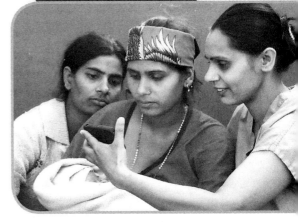

How to Weigh Information

Y̲ou land at night in a foreign country. No one around you speaks English. As you leave baggage claim, a man rushes up, blurts a babble of syllables, and urges you toward his car. Is he a taxi driver or a mugger?

It's hard when we're on someone else's turf and don't speak the language. The environmental debate puts us into a similar situation. We're vulnerable. But not helpless. First, we can learn the basic vocabulary—the goal of this book. Second, we can find trustworthy guides who *do* speak the language. But how do you know whom to trust?

Judging Media

All media aren't created equal.

Websites. Bloggers can put forth any opinion on any topic, with no qualifications required. The bio offered by the author might or might not be the whole truth. Industry money might be involved, as was revealed with the blog Watts Up With That. The Internet has made it easier than ever to be fooled.

It's also made it easier to figure out whether that's the case. Online text can give us live links to a writer's references, letting us check them out instantly. You'll see these in the bodies of articles and in the references at the end of most Wikipedia entries. A source that offers these links usually earns a higher reliability rating.

Take a look at those references. Some could be articles published by well-respected magazines. Others could lead down unlit streets to publishers and websites you've never heard of or up brightly lit boulevards maintained with corporate funds. Check them out. You can get a sense of online authors by the company they keep.

Expect lower standards at newspapers published solely online, where content might not be edited or verified. Like blogs, they often blur the line between news and opinion. At the same time, with the demise of many newspapers, much excellent journalism has moved online. The website Inside Climate News (insideclimatenews.com) won a 2013 Pulitzer Prize for its coverage of the underreported 2010 spill of Canadian tar sands oil in Marshall, Michigan.

Print newspapers and magazines. You're in safer territory here. Online sources are almost always free to readers, supported by ads or the organization maintaining the site; print media are funded by subscribers as well as ads. They therefore need to offer content and a reputation so good that readers will pay. This leads them to hire writers with journalism degrees and to pay editors to make sure all assertions are sound. *The New Yorker* magazine's fact-checkers are legendary. Opinion, clearly separated from news, is confined to personal columns and the editorial page.

This isn't to say that print media

are infallible or can give you the whole truth. With subscriptions down and ads and their revenue migrating online, the number of stories they can afford to pay for and print has shrunk dramatically. Writers might slip plagiarized or invented stories past editors, as has happened even at the venerable *New York Times*. Still, the bar is set higher here. Those writers of fraudulent stories were fired.

Professional journals.
Environmental writing will often reference papers published in *Science, Nature,* and more specialized journals. These get the highest reliability grade because they're peer-reviewed: checked by experts in the same field, something that junk science avoids. Not sure about an author? Check out where he or she has been published. Those whose work is published only by think tanks, for instance, but not in peer-reviewed journals are more likely to be peddling findings that wouldn't stand up to rigorous testing.

Books. Having one's opinions between the covers of a book has long conferred a respect that might or might not be justified. Publishers, like other print media outlets, need to make a profit, but books full of blather can sell in the millions. Think tanks churn out much junk science in book form. And self-published books, suddenly in reach of all, are as free of standards as blog posts. Again, check out the references and the author.

Documentaries. Making documentaries has gotten easier than ever before. So has showing them, courtesy of Netflix and streaming video. The advantage: we get coverage of topics that don't have enough commercial draw for the big screen. The downside: quality varies widely. Like bloggers, documentary makers tend to have a strong opinion on their subject and carefully edit in hopes you'll adopt it as your own. Material might be accurate, but expect black and white with very little gray.

Avoiding Being Fooled

Regardless of platform, be skeptical of statements backed up by nothing more than the writer's assurance. A Prius has a bigger carbon footprint than a Hummer due to the energy used to make it? Check it out before believing. The website snopes.com researches rumors of all sorts; Factcheck.org and similar sites do the same for claims in political ads and speeches.

Running background checks on every author and assertion takes a lot of work. Coming up with a group of news sources you trust will save on time. What else can you do to find them? Here are three recommendations from my own experience:

1. Follow the money. Checking for vested interests is the easiest way to eliminate pretenders. Businesses exist to sell products at a profit. Their perspective on the environment is, unsurprisingly, the one that will make them the most money. This makes sense. Looking to them for impartial data on pollution or climate doesn't. Buy your gas from Exxon, but get your science elsewhere. This means avoiding the individuals and groups they help fund.

How can you tell who's behind what you're reading? The same money that perverts science leaves fingerprints in the media. If you're not sure about a website or think tank mentioned in an article, see what the web tells you about its funding; SourceWatch.org has information on hundreds of front groups. To seem trustworthy, these groups hide the corporations that give them money. The makers of *Cool It* — a documentary that downplays climate fears and cutting carbon — refused to reveal their funding. This pointed the finger at the fossil-fuel lobby and dented the film's credibility. If a source hides its funding, assume it's tainted by money.

Think tanks that are fronts for industry will try to hide the names of businesses supporting them. The old method was to offer no funding info on their websites. The newer method: large donations from anonymous givers and from foundations — organizations that get funding from many sources and distribute it to many recipients. Laundering is the attempt to hide the source of something: drug cartels launder money; industries launder influence. In the mood for more detective work? Go to a foundation's website and see if the corporate donors are listed. A think tank that hides its money sources or sidesteps peer review shouldn't be trusted.

Scientists get paid. Why aren't their findings tainted? You'll find this argument all over the web to support labeling any worrisome climate data as junk science. To believe this charge, you'd have to believe in a conspiracy at institutions worldwide that demands researchers reach conclusions that condemn fossil fuels. There's been no credible evidence of this. By contrast, there's ample evidence that the fossil-fuel lobby has paid for results that dismiss greenhouse-gas worries. Branding climate researchers as junk scientists strikes me as a textbook case of projection.

2. Beware of mental vested interests. All vested interests aren't financial. Views on race and religion inspire fierce commitment without any connection to money. Once we adopt opinions, we're mentally invested and tend to close our eyes to information that would call our views into question. Questions bring doubt — an unwelcome mental visitor. And revising positions takes time and effort. It's easier to stick with what we've got.

The phenomenon of confirmation bias leads us to seek out and agree with information that supports our beliefs and to avoid what doesn't. With nothing to counter our opinions, we become overly sure of them and contemptuous of other views. If our information sources are similarly one-track, we won't be getting the whole picture.

As readers and viewers, we therefore need to not only check on a source's funding, but also to be wary of sources that project rock-solid certainty, a sign that the source may be too invested to be open to all the facts. Look for "might" and "could" and "possibly" instead of "will." Look for the grays that are everywhere in the real world but rare in political debate. Look for authors whose positions have changed to keep pace with the flow of new facts.

We need also to check that our own minds have remained open. Like junk scientists, we're all at risk of reasoning down from assumptions instead of up from facts. I began the book sure that all was lost, that unknown harmful feedback loops must lie all around us, that renewables couldn't possibly replace fossil fuels — none of which I'd examined closely. Some assumptions, like money's role in our fix, have stood up to the test. Others have not. The U.S. drought of 2012 may have had little to do with global warming. Recent findings have showed climate warming more slowly than expected despite rising greenhouse gases. Stay open to the facts, whatever they are.

3. Check for fallacies. The camera can lie, statistics can deceive, and words can be used to trick us into belief. Polar bear numbers are actually rising, but those who cite this as proof that global warming is a hoax are leaving out something crucial: the bears have increased not because warming is no problem but because the shooting of bears, which had brought their numbers low, was

restricted in the 1970s, allowing the population to spring back.

It was 2,500 years ago that the Greek philosopher Plato complained about speakers using fallacies — misleading verbal maneuvers that often sway audiences. Politicians have been making a living off of them ever since. A few examples:

The *ad hominem* argument: attacking an opponent rather than his or her position. "But what would you expect of someone with two DUI arrests?"

False dilemma: describing a situation as offering only two options. "You're either with us or against us."

Conspiracy theory: an unfounded belief in complex, secret plots. "All those tornadoes last month? The government seeded clouds and created them so then they could rush in and play the savior."

The appeal to emotion: relying on fear, pity, and other emotions instead of reason. "Lock your doors — Measure Q is coming!"

You see these fallacies and many more in use everywhere from your dining-room table to the State of the Union address. If this were football, a referee would throw a penalty flag. Since it's not, it's up to us to notice what's going on; the website flackcheck.org can help. You'll spot many verbal violations in the environmental debate. Recognizing them will help you decide which voices you can or can't rely on and will sharpen your skill at analyzing arguments in every realm.

Source Notes

Complete bibliographical information on sources not given here can be found in the Bibliography, beginning on page 176. When going to websites, be sure to omit the period that appears here after the URLs.

NOTICING
OPTICAL ILLUSIONS

p. 4 The planning fallacy   A Wikipedia search for
"cognitive biases" will give you a list so long you may forever doubt the name *Homo sapiens*.
Cordelia Fine's entertaining book *A Mind of Its Own* shows several of the most self-serving of
these fallacies in action.

p. 5 When the *Titanic* sank . . .   Finkelstein, p. 9.

p. 5 making leaps in agriculture, medicine, and a hundred other fields
James Burke's book *Connections* and the TV shows based on it show the pinball nature of
scientific knowledge, with discoveries ricocheting across the centuries and into other fields.

p. 5 pesticides killed many of the insects   The 2009 documentary *Vanishing of the
Bees* is one of many excellent treatments of the bee issue. The problem goes beyond bees to
insects in general and the birds who depend on them for food, all subject to powerful new
pesticides, habitat loss, and climate disruptions. When I moved to Aromas in 2002, the sky
held swallows by day and bats by night. Both depend on insects and both have disappeared.
That's just the view from my porch, but see http://www.ctpost.com/local/article/Shocking
-decline-seen-in-birds-that-eat-insects-4301848.php for a similar view from Connecticut. If
you're interested in birds and in contributing your observations, check out ebird.com, where
citizen scientists can post what they're seeing — findings that are included in the Fish and
Wildlife Service's annual U.S. State of the Birds report.

p. 5 This environmental news may . . .   McNeill, p. 4.

THE ESSENTIALS

POPULATION
p. 9 This huge population is flowing . . .   Brand, p. 25. For the reasons, see the
chapter "City Planet" in Brand. Alan Ehrenhalt's book *The Great Inversion and the Future of the
American City* (New York: Knopf, 2012) looks at the phenomenon in the United States, where
people are leaving the suburbs and returning to city centers for many of the same reasons.

p. 9 The year 2008 saw more people . . .   Brand, p. 25.

p. 9 For many reasons, urban families . . .   This fall in growth rate in more
developed countries is called the demographic transition. Among its causes: less need for
children's labor, greater chance children will survive childhood diseases, women's greater
access to education, and the availability of family planning help. See Brand, pp. 58–59, and
Gore, *The Future*, pp. 168–174.

p. 9 sometimes called the Third World   The origin of the term is unclear. Where's
the Second World, you ask? That referred to the Communist bloc nations after World
War II — the Soviet Union, Eastern Europe, and China — as opposed to the

industrialized capitalist nations of the First World. Everybody else fell into the Third World. Today, the term Newly Industrialized Countries (NICs) is often applied to India, China, Brazil, Indonesia, Malaysia, Mexico, and other rapidly developing nations.

p. 9 where four-fifths of the world lives   Worldwatch Institute, *Vital Signs 2010*, p. 24.

p. 9 The highest growth remains . . .   "Developing countries experiencing unprecedented growth, says UN report," United Nations News Centre website, http://www .un.org/apps/news/story.asp?NewsID=44371#.UaPl7Jwo3Kd. For more on the link between high population and poverty, see Diamond, pp. 511–512.

p. 9 Despite falling birth rates . . .   Gore, *The Future*, p. 166.

CONSUMPTION
p. 10 The West holds 20 percent   Clayton and Radcliffe, p. 209.

p. 11 Why isn't it sustainable?   See Diamond, pp. 494–496, for an overview of the sustainability of the Western lifestyle. Meadows et al. cover the topic at book length. The Ehrlichs' *One with Nineveh* (p. 82) estimates we'd need two more Earths to maintain our current lifestyle.

p. 11 Even critics of overconsumption   The exploits of Reverend Billy (the actor Bill Talen) and his troupe can be seen in the film *What Would Jesus Buy?*

p. 12 Heavy metals from computers . . .   Leonard, p. 203.

p. 12 Tiny particles of plastic . . .   See NOAA's excellent description of what garbage patches are and aren't at http://marinedebris.noaa.gov/info/patch.html. The Algalita Marine Research Institute (algalita.org) brings student involvement to the topic of plastic pollution.

p. 12 China's air pollution blows east . . .   Friedman, p. 404. See also the National Resource Defense Council's page at http://www.nrdc.org/health/effects/fasthma.asp.

p. 12 Sinks—the oceans, air, soil . . .   See Meadows et al., pp. 108–121, for a look into the planet's sinks.

ENERGY
p. 13 It takes thousands of coal cars . . .   Eric Lipton, "Even in Coal Country, the Fight for an Industry," *New York Times*, May 29, 2012, http://www.nytimes.com/2012/05/30/business /energy-environment/even-in-kentucky-coal-industry-is-under-siege.html?pagewanted=all.

p. 13 we drained the easily accessible supplies   See chapter 3 of Brown, *Plan B 4.0: Mobilizing to Save Civilization*.

p. 13 Cheap supplies do seem . . .   "The age of cheap energy is over." Nabuo Tanaka, executive director, International Energy Agency, 2011. Quoted in Inman. See following note.

p. 13 there's little net gain   EROI (energy returned on energy invested) figures have been declining for oil for decades, as we've been forced to pump less accessible and lower-quality supplies. Inman's *Scientific American* article has EROI estimates for liquid fuels as well as electricity sources. He puts tar sands at 5:1, just barely worth pursuing, and natural gas at 7:1. Solar comes in a 6:1, wind at 20:1. EROI varies depending on what's included, requires educated guessing, and isn't the whole story since it leaves out environmental impact — huge in the case of fossil fuels. Owen covers the subject on pp. 77–79 of *Green Metropolis*.

p. 13 Canadian tar sands and American shale oil Rachel Nuwer, "Oil Sands Mining Uses Up Almost as Much Energy as It Produces," *Inside Climate News* website, February 19, 2013, http://insideclimatenews.org/news/20130219/oil-sands-mining-tar-sands-alberta -canada-energy-return-on-investment-eroi-natural-gas-in-situ-dilbit-bitumen.

p. 14 scarcity is still an issue Klare, pp. 11–14.

p. 14 the largest in U.S. history The size of a spill doesn't always correlate with its impact. See "Gulf Leak: Biggest Spill May Not Be Biggest Disaster," *New Scientist* website, June 14, 2010, http://www.newscientist.com/article/dn19016-gulf-leak-biggest-spill-may -not-be-biggest-disaster.html.

p. 14 Burning coal puts dangerous mercury . . . Excellent descriptions of coal and its problems are offered by *National Geographic* (http://education.nationalgeographic .com/education/encyclopedia/coal/?ar_a=1) and the Union for Concerned Scientists (http://www.ucsusa.org/clean_energy/coalvswind/c02d.html).

p. 15 natural gas operations leak methane Jeff Tollefson, "Methane Leaks Erode Green Credentials of Natural Gas," *Nature* website, January 2, 2013, http://www.nature.com/news /methane-leaks-erode-green-credentials-of-natural-gas-1.12123. This claim has been challenged by a recent EPA report that found the methane problem negligible, though with the stakes so high and the EPA considered hopelessly compromised in the eyes of many environmentalists, its reports have been challenged in return. See "Limiting Methane Leaks Critical to Gas, Climate Benefits," *Climate Central* website, May 22, 2013, http://www.climatecentral.org/news/limiting- methane-leaks-critical-to-gas-climate-benefits-16020, for a look at both claims.

p. 15 Enough sunlight falls on the Earth U.S. Department of Energy, "Energy 101: Solar PV," 2011, http://www1.eere.energy.gov/multimedia/video_energy101_pv_text.html.

p. 15 Progress is being made Gore, *The Future*, pp. 342–344, 351–352. Brown, *World on the Edge*, chapter 9. These authors think the transition could be accomplished in a decade or two if we mobilized to achieve it. Others, like Brand (p. 307), feel that nuclear and clean coal will need to be added to conservation and renewables to give us enough energy.

p. 15 Texas, the top oil-producing . . . Brown, *World on the Edge*, p. 118.

p. 15 There's enough wind, solar . . . "The Energy Report," World Wildlife Fund, 2011, p. 23. http://wwf.panda.org/what_we_do/footprint/climate_carbon_energy/energy _solutions22/renewable_energy/sustainable_energy_report. See also Jacobson and Delucchi.

p. 15 suspected to have contaminated drinking water High stakes and vested interests have muddied the water on fracking's dangers to drinking water. Residents' complaints about polluted water have been countered by denials from energy companies, often backed up by state governments. The EPA did a U-turn on the issue in 2012, recanting its earlier warnings. See Jeff Tollefson's "Is Fracking behind Contamination in Wyoming Groundwater?" on *Nature*'s website (http://www.nature.com/news/is-fracking-behind -contamination-in-wyoming-groundwater-1.11543) as well as David Biello's "Fracking Can Be Done Safely, but Will It Be?" on *Scientific American*'s website (http://www.scientificamerican .com/article.cfm?id=can-fracking-be-done-without-impacting-water).

p. 15 A 2013 Stanford University study Elisabeth Rosenthal, "Life after Oil and Gas," *New York Times*, March 24, 2013, http://www.nytimes.com/2013/03/24/sunday

-review/life-after-oil-and-gas.html?pagewanted=all. The study about New York State can be read online at http://www.stanford.edu/group/efmh/jacobson/Articles/I /NewYorkWWSEnPolicy.pdf. See Jacobson and Delucci for an earlier study that looks at powering the whole world without fossil fuels.

p. 16 How the world's electricity is made "Key World Energy Statistics," International Energy Agency website, 2012, http://www.iea.org/publications /freepublications/publication/kwes.pdf.

p. 16 Turning plants into biofuels . . . Owen, *Green Metropolis,* pp. 77–79.

FOOD

p. 17 Scarcity of fresh water . . . and losing land to erosion Industrial agriculture's side effects on water and soil have been widely covered. See the website foodandwaterwatch.org and chapters 2 and 3 of Brown's *World on the Edge.*

p. 17 modern agriculture puts out more . . . "Agriculture and Food Production Contribute up to 29 Percent of Global Greenhouse Gas Emissions," *Science Daily* website, October 30, 2012, http://www.sciencedaily.com/releases/2012/10/121030210343.htm.

p. 18 antibiotics for animals The Worldwatch Institute's *Vital Signs 2010* (p. 60) states that 70 percent of U.S. antibiotics are fed to animals.

p. 18 our groundwater can contain pesticides and growth hormones For the U.S. Geological Survey's online fact sheets on water issues, including pesticides, see http://ga .water.usgs.gov/edu/pesticidesgw.html. For growth hormones, see Janet Raloff's article "Hormones: Here's the Beef" at *Science News* Online (http://www.phschool.com/science /science_news/articles/hormones_beef.html).

p. 18 nitrogen from fertilizers . . . Jonathan Mingle, "A Dangerous Fixation," *Slate,* March 12, 2013, http://www.slate.com/articles/health_and_science/the_efficient_planet /2013/03/nitrogen_fixation_anniversary_modern_agriculture_needs_to_use_fertilizer.html.

p. 18 antibiotics in milk and meat . . . David A. Kessler, "Antibiotics and the Meat We Eat." *New York Times,* March 27, 2013, http://www.nytimes.com/2013/03/28/opinion /antibiotics-and-the-meat-we-eat.html. See also the PBS show *Frontline*'s well-rounded coverage online at http://www.pbs.org/wgbh/pages/frontline/shows/meat/safe/overview.html.

p. 18 meat eating has tripled Worldwatch Institute, *Vital Signs 2012,* p. 12.

p. 18 an average ratio of seven to one Seven to one is my own averaging of the various estimates I came across, which ranged from 3:1 to 16:1. Different meat animals consume different amounts of grain.

p. 18 we're feeding half our grain . . . Worldwatch Institute, *Vital Signs 2010,* p. 60. For more on this topic, see Michael Pollan, "How to Feed the World," *Newsweek,* May 19, 2008, http://michaelpollan.com/articles-archive/how-to-feed-the-world.

p. 18 tropical forests are felled Bryan Walsh, "Meat: Making Global Warming Worse," *Time,* September 10, 2008, http://www.time.com/time/health/article/0,8599,1839995,00.html.

CLIMATE

p. 20 Scientists in the 1890s . . . The Swedish chemist Svante Arrhenius first predicted in 1896 that the CO_2 released from burned fossil fuels would raise temperature. For the fate of his theory over the next one hundred years, see Ian Sample's article "The Father of Climate Change," *Guardian,* June 30, 2005, www.guardian.co.uk/environment/2005/jun/30 /climatechange.climatechangeenvironment2.

p. 20 from spreading deserts to rising sea levels Elizabeth Kolbert's 2006 *Field Notes from a Catastrophe*, originally published in the *New Yorker*, was one of the first accounts of global warming outside of academic journals and remains one of the best. More recent data, maps, images, and explanations can be found, among many other places, at the climate page on NASA's website, http://climate.nasa.gov.

p. 20 we're headed for global disaster The IPCC's Assessment Reports give much evidence of this. These reports — drawing on several thousand peer-reviewed studies from scores of countries — present the findings of three working groups focused on the science of climate change, our options for adaptation, and mitigation strategies. A synthesis report draws these three strands together. The latest report is available online at ipcc.ch. Greenfacts.org offers a synopsis that's more easily digested without being cursory, with easy access to sources and further details; go to http://www.greenfacts.org/en/climate-change-ar4/index.htm#1. This book went to press before the IPCC's Fifth Assessment Report was released in its entirety.

p. 20 assigns a 95–100 percent likelihood See the IPCC website, ipcc.ch.

p. 20 the National Academy of Sciences, NASA For the NAS, see http://nas-sites .org/americasclimatechoices. For NASA, see climate.nasa.gov.

p. 20 the overwhelming majority of climatologists See Anderegg et al., which puts the number at 97–98 percent.

p. 20 will continue warming our climate for years Worldwatch Institute, *Vital Signs 2009*, p. 56.

p. 20 it begins to promote hurricanes McNeill, p. 4. NASA has good descriptions of tipping points and feedback loops at http://climate.nasa.gov/nasa_role/science.

p. 20 it's swerved suddenly in Earth's past Dumanoski, pp. 6–7, 79–80.

p. 20 on track to raise temperature 3.5°F Justin Gillis, "U.N. Climate Panel Endorses Ceiling on Global Emissions," *New York Times*, September 27, 2013.

p. 21 We've raised temperature 1.4° Friedman, p. 73. It's not always clear if the figure you read is in Celsius or Fahrenheit, since even American writers will often use Celsius but not necessarily add the identifying "C." When it's stated that we've raised temperature 1° since the start of the Industrial Revolution, that's Celsius (or an increase of 1.8°F). When you read that temperature rose 1° in the twentieth century, that's Fahrenheit (or an increase of .55°C). When the IPCC urges action to keep temperature from rising an additional 2°, that's Celsius (or an increase of 3.6°F). When it's mentioned that a drop of 5° was all it took to plunge the Earth into the last ice age, that's also Celsius (or a drop of 9°F).

PERCEPTION
VESTED INTERESTS

p. 29 would hire public relations (PR) firms   For a good look at how PR firms shape opinion, see Michael Krainish, "Washington's Robust Market for Attacks, Half-Truths," *Boston Globe*, May 19, 2013, http://www.bostonglobe.com/news/politics/2013/05/18/corporations -anonymously-fund-attacks-and-influence-washington-policy-through-nonprofit-groups /qyaJIFcv7yYOsQvya6ykAK/story.html.

p. 29 Galileo's observation of the stars . . .   Curiously, climate change skeptics and politicians have invoked Galileo as a fellow fighter against blind orthodoxy, forgetting that his cause was the validity of observation over belief.

p. 30 "I want you all . . . if we can."   UPI release, October 22, 1974, http://news.google .com/newspapers?nid=2245&dat=19741022&id=FJkzAAAAIBAJ&sjid=bzIHAAAAIBAJ& pg=6368,4649801.

p. 30 The Turkish government . . .   "Armenian Genocide," History.com website, http://www.history.com/topics/armenian-genocide.

p. 31 as happened to the Heartland Institute   Justin Gillis and Leslie Kaufman, "Leak Offers Glimpse of Campaign Against Climate Science," *New York Times*, February 15, 2012, http://www.nytimes.com/2012/02/16/science/earth/in-heartland-institute-leak-a -plan-to-discredit-climate-teaching.html?pagewanted=all&_r=0. DeSmogBlog.com, which first published the leaked documents, has more on Heartland's funding at http://www .desmogblog.com/heartland-institute.

p. 31 Citizens for Recycling First   "Citizens for Recycling First," The Center for Media and Democracy website, http://www.sourcewatch.org/index.php/Citizens_for_Recycling_First.

p. 31 The Greening Earth Society . . .   Pooley, p. 43.

p. 32 Global 500   CNN Money website, http://money.cnn.com/magazines/fortune /global500/2012/full_list/.

p. 32 their campaign is dwarfed   Christopher Doering, "Renewable Advocates Battle Oil Industry over Energy Policy," *USA Today*, July 2, 2012, http://usatoday30.usatoday.com /news/washington/story/2012-07-02/renewable-fuels-oil-congress/55987052/1.

p. 32 have invested trillions of dollars   Gore puts the figure at $7 trillion in *The Future*, p. 320.

p. 32 an estimated two thousand Washington lobbyists   Marianne Lavelle, "The Climate Change Lobby Explosion," Center for Public Integrity website, February 25, 2009, http://www.publicintegrity.org/node/4593.

p. 33 Producers of butter . . .   "Oleo Wars," Wisconsin Historical Society website. http://content.wisconsinhistory.org/cdm/compoundobject/collection/wmh/id/42291/ show/42227/rec/7.

COMMON SENSE

p. 36 Army Corps of Engineers . . . "Impossible Choice Faces America's First 'Climate Refugees,'" NPR website, May 18, 2013, http://www.npr.org/2013/05/18/185068648/impossible -choice-faces-americas-first-climate-refugees.

p. 37 Changes with fluctuations . . . Diamond, p. 425.

p. 37 average U.S. house size doubled . . . Margot Adler, "Behind the Ever-Expanding American Dream House," NPR website, http://www.npr.org/templates/story/story .php?storyId=5525283.

p. 38 Deforestation in Brazil is lowering . . . McKibben, *Eaarth*, p. 40.

p. 38 Midwest farming is causing fish . . . Agriculture's contribution to greenhouse gases is major, helping raise air temperature, which in turn has raised ocean temperature. Since fish and their food are adapted to specific temperatures, they've been changing their ranges to keep to the water that suits them.

p. 38 We like simple explanations . . . John Gertner, "Why Isn't the Brain Green?" *New York Times*, April 16, 2009, http://www.nytimes.com/2009/04/19/magazine/19Science-t .html?pagewanted=all&_r=0.

OUT OF SIGHT

p. 42 With only 2 percent of the U.S. population . . . National Institute of Food and Agriculture website, http://www.csrees.usda.gov/qlinks/extension.html.

p. 43 The vast majority of media . . . McChesney, pp. 28–30.

p. 43 "I find television . . . read a book." Groucho Marx, as quoted in Toni W. Aberson, *Compelling Conversations: Questions and Quotations on Timeless Topics* (Los Angeles, CA: Chimayo Press, 2010), p. 56.

p. 43 videos showing abusive treatment . . . Videos resulted in the nation's largest recall of beef from a Chino, California, slaughterhouse in 2008 and the closing of slaughterhouses in Grand Isle, Vermont, in 2009 and in Hanford, California, in 2012.

p. 43 That battle continues . . . Julie Jargon and Ian Berry, "Dough Rolls Out to Fight 'Engineered' Label on Food," *Wall Street Journal*, October 25, 2012, http://online.wsj .com/article/SB10001424052970203400604578073182907123760.html. The 2012 ballot proposition that would have required GMO labeling in California was defeated.

p. 43 In 2005 former vice president "The Halliburton Loophole," editorial, *New York Times*, November 2, 2009, http://www.nytimes.com/2009/11/03/opinion/03tue3.html.

p. 44 nearly three-quarters of Americans . . . Owen, *Green Metropolis*, p. 83. Seventy-two percent of the 501 respondents in the 2007 online survey were unaware of plastic's origins.

p. 44 *E. coli* outbreaks . . . William Neuman, "Outbreak in Europe May Revive Stalled U.S. Effort to Tighten Rules on Food Safety," *New York Times*, June 3, 2011, http://www.nytimes.com/2011/06/04/business/04prevent.html?pagewanted=all&_r=1&.

p. 44 The 9/11 attacks exposed . . . For more on the asbestos, mercury, lead, dioxins, and other toxins that populate buildings, see "2011 Annual Report on 9/11 Health,"

World Trade Center Medical Working Group of New York City, November, 2011, http://www
.nyc.gov/html/doh/wtc/downloads/pdf/news/wtc-mwg-annual-report2011.pdf#page=15.

IN THE NOW

p. 48 would cost up to twenty times   Walker and King, p. 148. Their chapter 10 has
an excellent discussion of the *Stern Review*. Nicholas Stern, its author, has since declared that
he underestimated the speed and seriousness of climate changes; see Heather Stewart and
Larry Elliot, "Nicholas Stern: 'I Got It Wrong on Climate Change — It's Far, Far Worse,'"
Guardian, January 26, 2013, http://www.guardian.co.uk/environment/2013/jan/27/nicholas
-stern-climate-change-davos.

p. 48 Aesop's fable   You can find the story at http://www.aesopfables.com/cgi/aesop1
.cgi?srch&fabl/TheAntandtheGrasshopper.

p. 48 Bangladesh foresaw population . . .   Bangladesh's attempt to control
population is less known and less successful than China's. See Nisha Kumar Kulkarni,
"Population Control and Urban Family Planning in Bangladesh," Searchlight South Asia
website, http://urbanpoverty.intellecap.com/?p=229.

p. 48 The Dutch plan for adapting . . .   Hertsgaard, p. 110.

p. 48 Many cultures have folktales . . .   This is motif #326 in the Aarne-Thompson
system. See "The Story of a Boy Who Went Forth to Learn Fear" in the Grimm brothers'
collection.

BACKSTORY: THE OIL EMBARGO

p. 50 It began with a surprise . . .   Information on the war, embargo, and its effects is
widely available. I recommend Merrill's brief book-length treatment, which includes speeches,
editorials, and other period documents.

p. 50 Only about one-tenth . . .   Quoted in Merrill, p. 64.

p. 51 the government demanded that Detroit . . .   Friedman, p. 42. Several things
about this are notable: how poor average gas mileage was before 1973, how quickly and
steeply Detroit improved it, and how advantageous it is to have a problem framed as a fight
against a foreign enemy.

p. 53 that America would defend . . .   "Let our position be absolutely clear: An
attempt by any outside force to gain control of the Persian Gulf region will be regarded as
an assault on the vital interests of the United States of America, and such an assault will be
repelled by any means necessary, including military force." Jimmy Carter, State of the Union
address, January 23, 1980. This became known as the Carter Doctrine.

DEFENSE MECHANISMS
DENIAL

p. 57 how we use defense mechanisms   Goleman has descriptions of some common
defense mechanisms on pp. 120–123.

p. 57 and began work on disconnecting . . .   See Wald for one of the campaign's
first forays.

Source Notes

p. 58 The vast majority of climate scientists . . .   See Anderegg et al.

p. 58 painted the issue . . .   The use of doubt to taint climate scientists' findings has been covered exhaustively in Oreskes and Conway's *Merchants of Doubt* among many books and articles on the topic. For a briefer and less academic treatment, I recommend Hoggan.

p. 58 to demand that their viewpoint be heard   Deniers have successfully used the appeal to fairness — "Let's hear both sides of the story" — to get media exposure for their views, even though scientists consider the case closed. State legislatures, school boards, and state textbook committees have all felt the pressure for "balanced" coverage in classrooms. For an overview of the school front, see Palmer. For a case involving the publisher Scholastic, see Bigelow.

p. 58 The lobby funds its own . . .   Pooley, pp. 39–43; Hoggan, pp. 73–84. Think tanks don't require of their authors relevant academic degrees or peer review. For a study of the books they publish and their authors' qualifications, see "Climate Change Denial Books and Conservative Think Tanks : Exploring the Connection," by Riley E. Dunlap and Peter J. Jacques, *American Behavioral Scientist*, May 14, 2013, http://abs.sagepub.com/content/57/6/699.full.pdf+html.

p. 58 Some of these are unqualified . . .   Hoggan, pp. 94–109; Pooley, pp. 33–44.

p. 59 Astroturf groups to give the appearance . . .   See chapter 4 in Hoggan for a full description.

p. 59 have paid PR firms to produce . . .   You can watch some of these among many fake news spots, most designed to sell products, at http://www.prwatch.org/fakenews2/findings/vnrs.

p. 59 Some fossil-fuel companies now state . . .   See ConocoPhillips's statement at http://www.conocophillips.com/sustainable-development/our-approach/living-by-our-principles /positions/Pages/climate-change.aspx.

p. 59 through anonymous donations   Suzanne Goldenberg, "Secret Funding Helped Build Vast Network of Climate Denial Thinktanks," *Guardian*, February 14, 2013, http://www .guardian.co.uk/environment/2013/feb/14/funding-climate-change-denial-thinktanks-network.

p. 59 sunspots, natural cycles . . .   See skepticalscience.com for a complete and well-annotated list.

p. 61 big-time problems out of the picture   Also left out is the fact that green energy creates jobs. It's hard to ascertain whether green energy tends to create more or fewer jobs than fossil fuels. See Bryan Walsh, "Green Jobs vs. Brown Jobs," *Time*, September 8, 2011, http://science.time.com/2011/09/08/green-jobs-vs-brown-jobs.

p. 61 Coal companies have funded . . .   See Hoggan (pp. 200–204) for a description of the campaign's founding. For a later update, see Anne Mulkern, "Coal Ad Blitz Launches New Spot as Industry Sees Political Gains," *New York Times*, February 8, 2010, http://www.nytimes.com/gwire/2010/02/08/08greenwire-coal-ad-blitz-launches -new-spot-as-industry-se-49401.html?pagewanted=all.

p. 61 the PR campaign painting wind and solar . . .   For a detailed report on this phenomenon and the money funding it, see "Clean Energy under Siege," Sierra Club website, http://www.sierraclub.org/pressroom/downloads/SierraClub-CleanEnergyUnderSiege.pdf.

p. 62 Its methods were developed . . .   Hertsgaard, pp. 258–60, Oreskes and Conway, chapter 1.

p. 62 Discrediting scientists and buying . . . Ross and Amter, p. 4.

p. 63 The United States is divided into . . . See Gore, *The Future*, pp. 317–319.

p. 63 a major motive to fall in line Some prominent Republicans defied this trend, like John McCain and California governor Arnold Schwarzenegger, who signed a landmark bill requiring the state to cut back on greenhouse gases. Most others sharing their views have kept quiet, but those no longer in office don't need to be and are hoping for a change. See Coral Davenport, "Retired Republicans Quietly Try to Shift GOP Climate-Change Focus," *National Journal* website, May 29, 2013, http://www.nationaljournal.com/energy/retired-republicans-quietly-try-to-shift-gop-climate-change-focus-20110930.

PROJECTION

p. 65 Individuals like to see . . . Fine's chapter "The Vain Brain" has much to say on this topic.

p. 65 have been termed terrorists "Many of the bills being introduced in statehouses across the U.S. have their origins in the conservative American Legislative Exchange Council, which has called those who interfere with animal operations terrorists and offered up sample legislation on this and other issues." Tracie Cone/Associated Press, "Calif. Bill to Thwart Animal Investigations Killed," *Charleston (WV) Daily Mail,* April 17, 2013, p. 9A.

p. 66 The several investigations . . . Sharon Begley, "Newspapers Retract 'Climategate' Claims, but Damage Still Done." *Newsweek/The Daily Beast,* June 25, 2010, http://www.newsweek.com/newspapers-retract-climategate-claims-damage-still-done-214472

p. 67 where TV meteorologists . . . Friedman, p. 175–178. See also Andrew Freedman, "NBC Fires Weather Channel Environmental Unit," *Washington Post* website, November 21, 2008, http://voices.washingtonpost.com/capitalweathergang/2008/11/nbc_fires_twc_environmental_un.html.

p. 67 A foreign threat . . . For a look at the demonization of foreign enemies, with hundreds of images of posters and cartoons from around the globe, see Sam Keen's *Faces of the Enemy: Reflections of the Hostile Imagination* (New York: Harper & Row, 1985).

p. 67 something our minds . . . Fine, pp. 28–29.

p. 67 "Be a good weather bimbo" Quoted in Friedman, p. 178.

REGRESSION

p. 70 Regression encourages the childish . . . Hall, p. 96.

p. 70 "If you really . . . lottery numbers" Homer Simpson, *The Simpsons,* "Kamp Krusty," Fox, 1992, Season 4, Episode no. 1.

p. 70 the makers of the Chinese . . . NetEase website, http://ir.netease.com/phoenix.zhtml?c=122303&p=irol-newsArticle&id=1820726.

p. 71 Surveyed Americans know more . . . Associated Press, "Study: More Know 'The Simpsons' than First Amendment Rights," *USA Today,* March 1, 2006, http://usatoday30.usatoday.com/news/nation/2006-03-01-freedom-poll_x.htm.

SYSTEMS
DEMOCRACY

p. 75 No more requesting sacrifice   A few headlines: "Both Parties Want No-Pain Power Solutions — Neither Wants to Follow Carter Lead and Call on Nation to Make Sacrifices," *Ventura County (CA) Star*, May 19, 2001. "Carter's Energy Plan — The Only Thing Politicians Learned from Carter's Disastrous 'Crisis of Confidence' Speech Is to Never Ask Americans to Sacrifice for Anything," *Gainesville Sun*, July 19, 2008. "Channeling Carter a Loser for Democrats," *Detroit News*, August 26, 2008.

p. 75 "I have nothing to offer . . . and sweat."   Winston Churchill, The Official Report, House of Commons (5th Series), 13 May 1940, vol. 360, c. 1502. On a day when the British were giving him more trouble than the Germans, the quotable Churchill summed up democracy as "the worst form of government except all the others that have been tried." In an even darker mood — one suspects after retirement from politics — he said, "The best argument against democracy is a five-minute conversation with the average voter."

p. 76 may soon be abolished   "Chinese Government Think Tank Urges End to Unpopular One-Child Policy." Behind the Wall/NBC News website, October 31, 2012, http://behindthewall.nbcnews.com/_news/2012/10/31/14830050-chinese-government -think-tank-urges-end-to-unpopular-one-child-policy?lite.

p. 77 and waged mainly with TV ads   Gore, *The Future*, pp. 63–66.

p. 77 out of public view until 2012   Brendan Greeley. "ALEC's Secrets Revealed; Corporations Flee," *Business Week*, May 3, 2012, http://www.businessweek.com/articles /2012-05-03/alecs-secrets-revealed-corporations-flee.

p. 77 They write legislation   Gore, *The Future*, pp. 104, 115.

p. 77 Innovations' birthplaces   Melosi, p. 221.

CAPITALISM

p. 80 European laws ban hundreds . . .   "European Laws," The Campaign for Safe Cosmetics website, http://safecosmetics.org/article.php?id=346.

p. 80 hobbled by business interests   Starving regulatory agencies for funding has succeeded in limiting their activities. See "Keep America's Food Safe: The Case for Increased Funding at FDA," Center for Science in the Public Interest website, http://www.cspinet.org /foodsafety/fdafunding.html. Changing, muffling, or ignoring findings that would impact industries has been common as well. See "Meddling at EPA? Activists Point to Survey," NBC News website, April 23, 2008, http://www.nbcnews.com/id/24276709/#.Ua4PKJzm-Spanish.

p. 80 has banned only a handful   Jim Avila, "FDA Regulation of Cosmetics Nears Despite Industry Objections," ABC News website, April 30, 2012, http://abcnews.go.com /blogs/lifestyle/2012/04/fdas-regulation-over-cosmetics-nears-despite-industry-backlash.

p. 81 releasing CO_2, reducing diversity . . .   "Palm Oil," World Wildlife Fund website, http://worldwildlife.org/industries/palm-oil.

p. 81 uprooting of half the world's . . .   Friedman, p. 82.

p. 81 because there was no immediate financial price . . .   Ibid., p. 236.

p. 81 banning logging after decades . . .   Diamond, p. 372.

p. 82 It's still fighting redemption . . .   For an example in Connecticut, see "More than $700,000 in Campaign Contributions Helped Sink the 'Bottle Bill'" on Common Cause's website, http://www.commoncause.org/site/apps/nl/content3.asp?c=dkLNK1MQIwG&b=263740&content_id={474AC9E1-413B-4F9F-935B-A2ADD81C029E}&notoc=1.

p. 82 If Home Depot demands . . .   Diamond, p. 477.

p. 83 Fossil-fuel companies receive . . .   Gore, *The Future*, pp. 342–343.

p. 83 that's what they'll do   This may already be happening in Australia. See "Renewable Energy Now Cheaper than New Fossil Fuels in Australia," Bloomberg /New Energy Finance website, February 7, 2013, http://about.bnef.com/press-releases /renewable-energy-now-cheaper-than-new-fossil-fuels-in-australia.

BACKSTORY: OZONE

p. 84 The crisis that resembled . . .   My summary is drawn from pp. 181–202 of Meadows et al. and from pp. 289–293 of Blatt. For a book-length account, see Roan.

p. 85 isn't expected to fully recover until late in the century   Blatt, pp. 292–293. NASA has an ozone page with constantly updated maps and more at ozonewatch.gsfc.nasa.gov.

ATTITUDES
SCIENCE TO THE RESCUE

p. 90 And hardware is much tougher . . .   Owen, *The Conundrum*, p. 218. See p. 251 for a discussion of the difficulties of switching to electric cars.

p. 90 When the bang we make . . .   Wright, p. 5. The author calls these "progress traps."

p. 91 DDT protected millions . . .   See Ross and Amter for an excellent look at DDT and the researchers who discovered the side effects of the many chemical compounds we've created.

p. 92 to worry about future problems   We've actually been tinkering with the world for millennia. See chapter 8 in Brand for an illuminating look at the effects of our learning to cultivate plants; the following chapter covers modern geoengineering.

p. 92 including shoes made by Puma   See c2ccertified.org.

p. 93 "Reality has a well-known liberal bias."   Stephen Colbert, White House Correspondents Association Dinner, April 29, 2006.

NEVER RETREAT

p. 96 "A man is rich . . . to let alone"   Henry David Thoreau, in *Walden* (Cambridge, MA: The University Press, 1910), p. 118.

p. 97 Bluefin tuna is in steep decline   Kurlansky, p. 167.

p. 97 we're draining them faster   Meadows et al., p. 71.

Source Notes

p. 97 At the first international climate summit Philip Elmer-DeWitt, "Summit to Save the Earth: Rich vs. Poor," *Time*, June 1, 1992. Online at http://content.time.com/time /magazine/article/0,9171,975656-1,00.html.

p. 99 The Transition movement See transitionus.org.

p. 101 the twenty or so other strains . . . Dumanoski, pp. 100–101.

p. 101 Use of mass transit goes up . . . Owen, *Green Metropolis*, p. 133.

NO LIMITS

p. 103 Geography has left an imprint . . . The idea that the United States, Canada, and Australia are linked in some of their behaviors (and the term the Big Three) comes from no source other than my own observation, though the notion may have been planted by this description I chanced upon, written by a Briton visiting a North Carolina beach: "Such a beach would be inconceivable in Europe. There is nothing tight or contained about it. It is sheer extent. You could see the whole history of America — its amazement at the natural wonders of the new world; its extraordinary indifference to its desecration of them — as the simple product of minds used to the constraints of Europe meeting this sort of unconstraint, the sheer extravagance of natural form, the hugeness of gesture which makes up America." Adam Nicolson, *On Foot: Guided Walks in England, France, and the United States* (New York: Harmony Books, 1990), p. 79.

p. 103 Europe was largely deforested Hughes, pp. 88–94.

p. 104 there's always more around the bend David Potter's *People of Plenty: Economic Abundance and the American Character* (Chicago: University of Chicago Press, 1954) is the classic study of this with regard to the United States.

p. 104 Population density per square mile "File: Population and population density, 1960 and 2012," Eurostat website, http://epp.eurostat.ec.europa.eu/statistics_explained /index.php?title=File:Population_and_population_density,_1960_and_2012.png&filetime stamp=20130130111941.

p. 104 there aren't enough riders . . . Owen, *Green Metropolis*, p. 120.

p. 104 Per capita CO_2 emissions "CO_2 emissions (metric tons per capita)," World Bank website, http://data.worldbank.org/indicator/EN.ATM.CO2E.PC.

p. 105 leading the way in researching . . . Damian Carrington, "Whatever Happened to Carbon Capture in the Fight against Climate Change?" *Guardian*, May 9, 2012, http://www.guardian.co.uk/environment/2012/may/09/carbon-capture-storage-climate -change?INTCMP=SRCH.

p. 107 Rising water temperature . . . For a good look at the reef, see *National Geographic's* story in the May 2011 issue, online at http://ngm.nationalgeographic .com/2011/05/great-barrier-reef/holland-text.

p. 107 "All politics is local." Tip O'Neill, in his primer on politics, *All Politics Is Local: and Other Rules of the Game* (New York: Crown Books, 1993).

LOSING CONTROL

p. 110 "If the U.S. Environmental . . . insolvent."   Roland Hwang and Matt Peak, *Innovation and Regulation in the Automobile Sector*, p. 2, National Resources Defense Council website, http://docs.nrdc.org/air/files/air_08030301A.pdf.

p. 110 None of his predictions . . .   Friedman, pp. 327–328.

p. 110 Seat belts, turn signals . . .   See Richard Byrne, "Life in the Slow Lane: Tracking Decades of Automaker Roadblocks to Fuel Economy," Union of Concerned Scientists website, July 2003, http://www.ucsusa.org/clean_vehicles/smart-transportation-solutions /better-fuel-efficiency/life-in-the-slow-lane.html.

p. 111 new challenges have often . . .   Friedman, pp. 328–330; Meadows et al., pp. 199–201.

p. 112 Japan, Norway, and Iceland . . .   "Whaling," Greenpeace website, http://www .greenpeace.org/international/en/campaigns/oceans/whaling.

BACKSTORY: KYOTO

p. 114 The first United Nations summit . . .   Information on the Kyoto Protocol is widely available. I recommend Kolbert, chapter 8, and Leggett, chapter 11, which give eyewitness accounts of the negotiations, which were attended by more lobbyists than government representatives.

p. 115 lobbied American politicians   Kolbert, p. 156.

p. 117 more than 70,000 deaths   "Climate Change and Health," World Health Organization website, October 2012, http://www.who.int/mediacentre/factsheets/fs266/en.

p. 117 the United States and China working together to block progress   Gerald Trauffetter, "Copenhagen Climate Cables: The US and China Joined Forces against Europe," *Spiegel Online International,* December 8, 2010, http://www.spiegel.de/international/world /copenhagen-climate-cables-the-us-and-china-joined-forces-against-europe-a-733630.html.

EYES ABROAD AND AHEAD
CONFLICT

p. 120 Even nations with no Arctic . . .   Elizabeth Rosenthal, "Race Is On as Ice Melt Reveals Arctic Treasures," *New York Times,* September 18, 2012, http://www.nytimes .com/2012/09/19/science/earth/arctic-resources-exposed-by-warming-set-off-competition .html?pagewanted=all.

p. 121 Mars, a god of crops . . .   McDonough and Braungart, *Cradle to Cradle*, p. 94.

p. 121 Britain colonized . . .   Richards, pp. 221–227. Forests covered only one-tenth of Great Britain in the sixteenth century, with a growing population bringing growing demands on them for fuel and clearing them for food and pasture, forcing Britain to look to North America and the Baltic region for wood. As her forests reached the point of exhaustion in the eighteenth century, Britain was spurred to convert to a new fuel source: coal.

p. 122 Weapons are their most popular offering   Klare, p. 7.

Source Notes

p. 122 China's attempt to buy . . . Ibid., pp. 1–6.

p. 123 The Caspian Sea region . . . See chapter 5 in Klare for a full description.

p. 123 Such jackpots have often . . . Humphreys et al., pp. 1–2.

p. 124 It's no accident that the world's . . . Diamond, pp. 515–516.

p. 124 These conditions helped lead to the genocide . . . Ibid., pp. 311–328.

p. 125 the cause of thousands of deaths Lester R. Brown, "When Population Growth and Resource Availability Collide," Earth Policy Institute website, February 12, 2009, http://www.earth-policy.org/book_bytes/2009/pb3ch06_ss5.

p. 125 have exploded in Nigeria Ibid.

p. 127 led more than two million people . . . Wooster, p. 49.

p. 127 Los Angeles sent a "bum brigade" . . . Walters, p. 26.

p. 127 disasters that never had to be cleaned up For an American instance of good stewardship that reversed the fortunes of a much-loved body of water, see Stephen R. Palumbi and Carolyn Sotka, *The Death and Life of Monterey Bay: A Story of Revival* (Washington, DC: Island Press, 2011).

CHINDIA

p. 129 caused a wobble "Three Gorges Dam and the Earth's Rotation," Energy Library website, http://www.theenergylibrary.com/node/11435.

p. 130 puts it on track to pass China Meredith, p. 132.

p. 131 is expected to be passed by China's Brett Arends, "IMF Bombshell: Age of America Nears End," MarketWatch.com website, April 25, 2011, http://articles.marketwatch.com /2011-04-25/commentary/30714377_1_imf-chinese-economy-international-monetary-fund.

p. 131 This push has caused . . . Friedman, p. 400; Klare, pp. 70–71, 80–81.

p. 132 all combine to transform a country's . . . Owen has described this phenomenon well. See pp. 101–105 in *Green Metropolis* and pp. 65–67 in *The Conundrum*.

p. 132 China is predicted to top . . . "Worldwatch Report: Powering China's Development," Worldwatch Institute website, http://www.worldwatch.org/node/5491.

p. 132 that they can last days Peter Ford, "China Traffic Jam Enters Day 11. A Tale of Deceit and Criminality?" *Christian Science Monitor*, August 24, 2010, http://www.csmonitor .com/World/Global-News/2010/0824/China-traffic-jam-enters-Day-11.-A-tale-of-deceit -and-criminality.

p. 132 must now scour the world . . . Klare, p. 64.

p. 133 despite its downsides Ibid., pp. 74–75.

p. 133 have produced "cancer villages" Tom Phillips, "China Admits Pollution Has Caused 'Cancer Villages,'" *Telegraph*, February 22, 2013, http://www.telegraph.co.uk/news /worldnews/asia/china/9887413/China-admits-pollution-has-caused-cancer-villages.html.

p. 133 The boom in refrigeration . . . Keith Bradsher, "The Price of Keeping Cool in Asia; Use of Air-Conditioning Refrigerant Is Widening the Hole in the Ozone Layer," *New York Times*, February 23, 2007, http://query.nytimes.com/gst/fullpage.html?res=9804EFDD1 03EF930A15751C0A9619C8B63&pagewanted=all.

p. 133 demand for disposable chopsticks Rachel Nuwer, "Disposable Chopsticks Strip Asian Forests," *New York Times*, October 24, 2011, http://green.blogs.nytimes.com /2011/10/24/disposable-chopsticks-strip-asian-forests.

p. 133 China recently passed the United States . . . McKibben, *Eaarth*, p. 79.

p. 133 India is currently number three "World Carbon Emissions: The League Table of Every Country," *Guardian*, http://www.guardian.co.uk/environment/datablog/2012 /jun/21/world-carbon-emissions-league-table-country.

p. 134 global warming is taken seriously there Thomas Friedman, "Aren't We Clever?" *New York Times*, September 18, 2010, http://www.nytimes.com/2010/09/19 /opinion/19friedman.html?ref=thomaslfriedman&_r=0. Indians aren't nearly as unanimous, those rejecting the claim tending to see in it American desire to hold back their economy.

p. 134 India has placed a carbon tax on coal "Carbon Tax and Emissions Trading: How Countries Compare," *Guardian*, July 10, 2011, http://www.guardian.co.uk/environment /2011/jul/10/carbon-tax-emissions-trading-international.

p. 134 riders of gas-powered scooters . . . Friedman, p. 420.

p. 134 allowing prices so low . . . Nathaniel Austin, "China, U.S. Butt Heads over Green Energy," *The Diplomat*, September 22, 2012, http://thediplomat.com/china-power /china-u-s-butt-heads-over-green-energy.

p. 135 The "Green Wall of China" For more on this, see Mitch Moxley, "China's Great Green Wall Grows in Climate Fight," *Guardian*, September 23, 2010, http://www.guardian .co.uk/environment/2010/sep/23/china-great-green-wall-climate.

p. 135 the average Indian . . . Union of Concerned Scientists website, http://www .ucsusa.org/global_warming/science_and_impacts/science/each-countrys-share-of-co2.html.

FIXES

p. 139 turns out to be a more important gauge . . . Owen, *Green Metropolis*, p. 300.

p. 139 a modest help rather than a cure-all Ibid., pp. 296–297. See the books by William McDonough and Michael Braun for much more on this topic.

p. 139 perpetuates car use This is called the Jevons paradox (or Jevons effect). Owen discusses it in detail in pp. 103–145 of *The Conundrum*.

p. 139 Because of fraud Doug Struck, "Buying Carbon Offsets May Ease Eco-guilt but Not Global Warming," *Christian Science Monitor*, April 20, 2010, http://www.csmonitor.com /Environment/2010/0420/Buying-carbon-offsets-may-ease-eco-guilt-but-not-global-warming.

Source Notes

COMING SOON

p. 143 worrisome figures have usually outstripped projections   See "Key Scientific Developments Since the IPCC Fourth Assessment Report," Center for Climate and Energy Solutions website, June 2009, http://www.pewclimate.org/docUploads /Key-Scientific-Developments-Since-IPCC-4th-Assessment.pdf. Better news arrived in 2013: see Alex Kirby and The Daily Climate, "Is Global Warming Cooler than Expected?" *Scientific American* website, May 24, 2013, http://www.scientificamerican.com/article .cfm?id=is-global-warming-cooler-than-expected&page=2.

p. 143 may even welcome environmental collapse   See, for example, the Global Warming page at Born Again Christian's website: http://www.born-again-christian.info /views/christian-perspective-on-climate-change.htm.

p. 143 Nonreligious people may say it . . .   For an example, see Dumanoski, pp. 96–97. Brand has an excellent discussion of doomsaying's long tradition on pp. 210–13.

p. 145 or switch to biomass   Is burning trees a good thing? See "Forests Not Fuels," National Resources Defense Council website, August 2011, http://www.nrdc.org/energy /forestsnotfuel/files/forests-not-fuel.pdf.

p. 145 More than half of U.S. states . . .   See Friedman, pp. 304–305 for more on portfolios. For a list of state requirements current as of 2010, go to http://www.ncsl.org /issues-research/energyhome/state-renewable-portfolio-standards.aspx.

p. 145 In Australia, it's now cheaper . . .   "Renewable Energy Now Cheaper than New Fossil Fuels in Australia," Bloomberg New Energy Finance, February 7, 2013, http://about.bnef .com/press-releases/renewable-energy-now-cheaper-than-new-fossil-fuels-in-australia/.

p. 146 "History teaches us . . . alternatives."   Abba Eban, in a speech in London on December 16, 1970, as quoted in *The Times* (London), December 17, 1970.

p. 147 The Dutch are relocating . . .   Michael Kimmelman, "Going with the Flow," *New York Times*, February 13, 2013, http://www.nytimes.com/2013/02/17/arts/design /flood-control-in-the-netherlands-now-allows-sea-water-in.html?_r=0.

p. 147 Peru is experimenting . . .   Gore, *The Future*, p. 357.

p. 147 make money selling credits   Andrew Clark, "Exxon Chief Backs Carbon Tax," *Guardian*, January 9, 2009, http://www.guardian.co.uk/business/2009/jan/10/exxon-mobil -carbon-tax.

p. 148 since that's how two-thirds . . .   U.S. Energy Information Agency website, http:// www.eia.gov/tools/faqs/faq.cfm?id=427&t=3. In 2012, the power sources for U.S. electricity were coal, 37%; natural gas, 30%; nuclear, 19%; hydropower, 7%; renewables and others, 7%.

p. 148 The added cost of carbon capture . . .   Gore, *The Future*, pp. 353–354.

p. 149 we've rediscovered the benefits . . .   Alan Ehrenhalt, "Cities of the Future May Soon Look Like Those of the Past," Governing website, April 2012, http://www.governing .com/topics/economic-dev/gov-cities-of-future-may-soon-look-like-past.html.

p. 150 eight climate-related disasters   Gore, *The Future*, p. 346.

p. 150 2012 brought eleven   "Preliminary Info on 2012 U.S. Billion-Dollar Extreme Weather/Climate Events," NOAA website, http://www.ncdc.noaa.gov/news/preliminary-info -2012-us-billion-dollar-extreme-weatherclimate-events.

p. 151 ruling groups are usually . . .   See Diamond's chapter 14 for many examples and a discussion of the reasons behind disastrous decisions.

p. 151 The more leaders are protected . . .   Diamond, p. 341.

p. 152 future drilling in the Arctic, Africa, Asia . . .   Klare has full chapters on Africa and Asia. For a glimpse of the Arctic, see Mike Shuster, "To Tap Arctic Oil, Russia Partners with Exxon Mobil," NPR website, May 25, 2012, http://www.npr .org/2012/05/25/153603820/to-tap-arctic-oil-russia-partners-with-exxon-mobil.

p. 152 Nuclear power has been embraced   James Lovelock, who formulated the Gaia theory, is probably the most prominent. See chapter 4 in Brand for a report on this shift.

p. 152 led to millions of deaths   Brand, p. 219.

p. 153 Three-quarters of the world now uses cell phones   Gore, *The Future*, p. 53.

p. 153 One-third of the world is now connected to the Internet   Ibid.

HOW TO WEIGH INFORMATION

p. 154 the blog Watts Up With That   Leo Hickman, "Climate Sceptics — Who Gets Paid What?" *Guardian*, February 15, 2012, http://www.guardian.co.uk/environment/2012 /feb/15/climate-sceptics-pai-heartland-institute.

p. 155 Think tanks churn out much junk science   Graham Readfearn, "Research Reveals Almost All Climate Science Denial Books Linked to Conservative Think Tanks," DeSmogBlog website, March 20, 2013, http://www.desmogblog.com/2013/03/20/research -reveals-almost-all-climate-science-denial-books-linked-conservative-think-tanks.

p. 156 The makers of *Cool It* . . . refused to reveal their funding   Robert Collier, "Bjorn Lomborg Film Offers New Convenient Truth," *San Francisco Chronicle*, November 7, 2010, http://www.sfgate.com/green/article/Bjorn-Lomborg-film-offers-new-convenient -truth-3167034.php#ixzz1jx2lJqGP.

p. 156 the fossil-fuel lobby has paid for results that dismiss greenhouse-gas worries   Hoggan, pp. 94–109; Pooley, pp. 33–44.

p. 157 but because the shooting of bears   Zac Unger, *Never Look a Polar Bear in the Eye: A Family Field Trip to the Arctic's Edge in Search of Adventure, Truth, and Mini-Marshmallows* (Cambridge, MA: Da Capo Press, 2013), p. 186.

p. 157 The government seeded clouds . . .   See Sam Prince, "Oklahoma Tornado Conspiracy Theories: 5 Fast Facts You Need to Know," Heavy.com website, May 22, 2013, http://www.heavy.com/news/2013/05/oklahoma-tornado-conspiracy-theories.

Bibliography

BOOKS AND ARTICLES

Anderegg, William R. L., et al. "Expert Credibility in Climate Change." *Proceedings of the National Academy of Sciences of the United States of America*. 107 (27), July 6, 2010. http://www.pnas.org/content/early/2010/06/04/1003187107.full.pdf+html.

Aronson, Marc, and Marina Budhos. *Sugar Changed the World: A Story of Magic, Spice, Slavery, Freedom, and Science.* New York: Clarion, 2010.

Bigelow, Bill. "Scholastic Inc.: Pushing Coal." *Rethinking Schools*, summer 2011. http://www.rethinkingschools.org/archive/25_04/25_04_bigelow2.shtml.

Blatt, Harvey. *America's Environmental Report Card*, 2d ed. Cambridge, MA: MIT Press, 2011.

Brand, Stewart. *Whole Earth Discipline: Why Dense Cities, Nuclear Power, Transgenic Crops, Restored Wildlands, and Geoengineering Are Necessary.* New York: Penguin, 2010.

Brown, Lester R. *Plan B 4.0: Mobilizing to Save Civilization.* New York: Norton, 2009. http://www.earth-policy.org/images/uploads/book_files/pb4book.pdf.

———. *World on the Edge.* New York: Norton, 2011. http://www.earth-policy.org/images /uploads/book_files/wotebook.pdf.

Burgeson, John. "Shocking Decline Seen in Birds That Eat Insects in Flight." CTPost.com, February 22, 2013. http://www.ctpost.com/local/article/Shocking-decline-seen-in-birds -that-eat-insects-4301848.php.

Burke, James. *Connections.* New York: Simon and Schuster, 2007.

Campbell, Neil A., and Jane B. Reece. *Biology*, 8th ed. Upper Saddle River, NJ: Pearson, 2008.

Catton, William R. *Overshoot: The Ecological Basis of Revolutionary Change.* Champaign, IL: University of Illinois Press, 1982.

Clayton, Tony, and Nicholas Radcliffe. *Sustainability: A Systems Approach.* New York: Routledge, 1996.

Cline, Elizabeth L. *Overdressed: The Shockingly High Cost of Cheap Fashion.* New York: Penguin, 2012.

Cohen, Joel E. *How Many People Can the Earth Support?* New York: Norton, 1995.

de Graff, John, David Wann, and Thomas H. Naylor. *Affluenza: The All-Consuming Epidemic.* San Francisco: Berrett-Koehler, 2001.

Diamond, Jared. *Collapse: How Societies Choose to Fail or Succeed.* New York: Viking, 2005.

Dobb, Edwin. "America Strikes New Oil." *National Geographic*, March 2013, pp. 28–59. http://ngm.nationalgeographic.com/2013/03/bakken-shale-oil/dobb-text.

Dumanoski, Dianne. *The End of the Long Summer: Why We Must Remake Our Civilization to Survive on a Volatile Earth.* New York: Crown, 2009.

Ehrlich, Paul R. *The Population Explosion.* New York: Simon and Schuster, 1990.

Ehrlich, Paul R., and Anne H. Ehrlich. *One with Nineveh: Politics, Consumption, and the Human Future*. Washington, DC: Island Press, 2005.

———. "The Population Bomb Revisited." *Electronic Journal of Sustainable Development*, I (3), 2009. http://www.populationmedia.org/wp-content/uploads/2009/07/Population-Bomb -Revisited-Paul-Ehrlich-20096.pdf.

Fine, Cordelia. *A Mind of Its Own: How Your Brain Distorts and Deceives*. New York: Norton, 2006.

Finkelstein, Norman H. *Plastics*. Tarrytown, NY: Marshall Cavendish, 2008.

Friedman, Thomas L. *Hot, Flat, and Crowded*. New York: Picador, 2009.

Goleman, Daniel. *Vital Lies, Simple Truths: The Psychology of Self-Deception.* New York: Simon and Schuster, 1985.

Goodell, Jeff. *How to Cool the Planet: Geoengineering and the Audacious Quest to Fix Earth's Climate*. Boston: Houghton Mifflin Harcourt, 2010.

Gore, Al. *Our Choice: A Plan to Solve the Climate Crisis*. New York: Rodale, 2009.

———. *The Future: Six Drivers of Global Change*. New York: Random House, 2013.

Hall, Calvin S. *A Primer of Freudian Psychology*. New York: World Publishing, 1954.

Hawken, Paul. *Blessed Unrest: How the Largest Movement in the World Came into Being, and Why No One Saw It Coming*. New York: Viking, 2007.

Hertsgaard, Mark. *Hot: Living through the Next Fifty Years on Earth*. Boston: Houghton Mifflin Harcourt, 2011.

Hoggan, James. *Climate Cover-Up: The Crusade to Deny Global Warming*. Vancouver: Greystone, 2009.

Hughes, J. Donald. *An Environmental History of the World*. New York: Routledge, 2009.

Humphreys, Macartan, Jeffrey D. Sachs, and Joseph Eugene Stiglitz, eds. *Escaping the Resource Curse*, New York: Columbia University Press, 2007.

Inman, Mason. "The True Costs of Fossil Fuels." *Scientific American*, April 2013, pp. 59–62. Sources for the author's figures are online at http://www.scientificamerican.com/article .cfm?id=eroi-behind-numbers-energy-return-investment&page=2.

Jacobson, Mark Z., and Mark A. Delucci. "A Plan to Power 100 Percent of the Planet with Renewables." *Scientific American*, November 2009. http://www.scientificamerican.com /article.cfm?id=a-path-to-sustainable-energy-by-2030.

Kahn, Lloyd. *Tiny Homes: Simple Shelter*. Bolinas, CA: Shelter Publications, 2012.

Klare, Michael T. *Rising Powers, Shrinking Planet: The New Geopolitics of Energy*. New York: Metropolitan Books, 2008.

Kolbert, Elizabeth. *Field Notes from a Catastrophe: Man, Nature, and Climate Change*. New York: Bloomsbury, 2006.

Kurlansky, Mark. *World without Fish*. New York: Workman, 2011.

Lappé, Anna. *Diet for a Hot Planet: The Climate Crisis at the End of Your Fork and What You Can Do about It*. New York: Bloomsbury, 2011.

LeBlanc, Steven A. *Constant Battles: The Myth of the Peaceful, Noble Savage*. New York: St. Martin's, 2003.

Leggett, Jeremy. *Carbon War: Global Warming and the End of the Oil Era*. New York: Routledge, 2001.

Leonard, Annie. *The Story of Stuff: How Our Obsession with Stuff Is Trashing the Planet, Our Communities, and Our Health — and a Vision for Change*. New York: Free Press, 2010.

Lynas, Mark. *Six Degrees: Our Future on a Hotter Planet*. Washington, DC: National Geographic, 2008.

MacDougall, J. D. *A Short History of Planet Earth: Mountains, Mammals, Fire, and Ice*. New York: Wiley, 1998.

McChesney, Robert W. *Rich Media, Poor Democracy: Communication Politics in Dubious Times*. Urbana, IL: University of Illinois Press, 1999.

McDonough, William, and Michael Braungart. *Cradle to Cradle: Remaking the Way We Make Things*. New York: North Point, 2002.

———. *The Upcycle: Beyond Sustainability — Designing for Abundance*. New York: North Point, 2013.

McKibben, Bill. *Eaarth: Making a Life on a Tough New Planet*. New York: Times Books, 2010.

———. *The End of Nature*. New York: Random House, 1989.

———. "Global Warming's Terrifying New Math." *Rolling Stone*, August 2012. http://www
.rollingstone.com/politics/news/global-warmings-terrifying-new-math-20120719.

McNeill, J. R. *Something New under the Sun: An Environmental History of the Twentieth-Century World*. New York: Norton, 2000.

Meadows, Donella, Jorgen Randers, and Dennis Meadows. *Limits to Growth: The 30-Year Update*. White River Junction, VT: Chelsea Green, 2004.

Melosi, Martin V. *Garbage in the Cities: Refuse, Reform, and the Environment*. College Station, TX: Texas A&M University Press, 1981.

Meredith, Robyn. *The Elephant and the Dragon*. New York: Norton, 2007.

Merrill, Karen R. *The Oil Crisis of 1973–1974 : A Brief History with Documents*. Boston: Bedford/St. Martin's, 2007.

Oreskes, Naomi, and Erik M. Conway. *Merchants of Doubt: How a Handful of Scientists Obscured the Truth on Issues from Tobacco Smoke to Global Warming*. New York: Bloomsbury, 2010.

Owen, David. *Green Metropolis: Why Living Smaller, Living Closer, and Driving Less Are the Keys to Sustainability*. New York: Riverhead, 2009.

———. *The Conundrum: How Scientific Innovation, Increased Efficiency, and Good Intentions Can Make Our Energy and Climate Problems Worse*. New York: Riverhead, 2011.

Palmer, Lisa. "Public Schools' Global Warming Teachings: A Rich Field for Mining for News Stories," Yale Forum on Climate Change and the Media website, http://www
.yaleclimatemediaforum.org/2010/06/teaching-climate-change-as-edu-news-beat.

Pollan, Michael. "Power Steer." *New York Times Magazine*, March 21, 2002, http://www
.nytimes.com/2002/03/31/magazine/power-steer.html?pagewanted=all&src=pm.

———. *The Omnivore's Dilemma*. New York: Penguin, 2006.

Pooley, Eric. *The Climate War: True Believers, Power Brokers, and the Fight to Save the Earth*.
New York: Hyperion, 2010.

Regis, Ed. "The Doomslayer." *Wired*, February 1997. www.wired.com/wired/archive/5.02
/ffsimon_pr.html.

Richards, John F. *The Unending Frontier: An Environmental History of the Early Modern World*.
Berkeley, CA: University of California Press, 2003.

Roan, Sharon L. *Ozone Crisis*. New York: Wiley, 1989.

Ross, Benjamin, and Steven Amter. *The Polluters: The Making of Our Chemically Altered
Environment*. New York: Oxford University Press, 2010.

Schlosser, Eric. *Fast Food Nation: The Dark Side of the All-American Meal*. Boston:
Houghton Mifflin, 2001.

Schlosser, Eric, and Charles Wilson, *Chew on This: Everything You Don't Want to Know about
Fast Food*. Boston: Houghton Mifflin Harcourt, 2007.

"Stabilization Wedges Introduction." Carbon Mitigation Initiative. July 27, 2011. Princeton
University. Retrieved May 11, 2013. http://cmi.princeton.edu/wedges/intro.php.

Stager, Curt. *Deep Future: The Next 100,000 Years of Life on Earth*. New York: St. Martin's, 2012.

Tuchman, Barbara. *The March of Folly: From Troy to Vietnam*. New York: Knopf, 1984.

Wald, Matthew L. "Pro-Coal Ad Campaign Disputes Warming Idea," *New York Times*, July 8,
1991, http://www.nytimes.com/1991/07/08/business/pro-coal-ad-campaign-disputes
-warming-idea.html.

Walker, Gabriela, and David King. *The Hot Topic: What We Can Do about Global Warming*.
Orlando, FL: Harvest, 2008.

Walters, Dan. *California: Facing the 21st Century*. Sacramento, CA: California Journal Press,
1992.

Wooster, Daniel. *Dust Bowl: The Southern Plains in the 1930s*. New York: Oxford University
Press, 1979.

Worldwatch Institute. *Vital Signs 2009*. Washington, DC: Worldwatch Institute, 2009.

———. *Vital Signs 2010*. Washington, DC: Worldwatch Institute, 2010.

———. *Vital Signs 2011*. Washington, DC: Worldwatch Institute, 2011.

———. *Vital Signs 2012*. Washington, DC: Worldwatch Institute, 2012.

Wright, Ronald. *A Short History of Progress*. Cambridge, MA: Da Capo Press, 2005.

Bibliography

VIDEOS

(Astro)Turf Wars. Directed by Taki Oldman. Abbotsford, Victoria, Australia: Larrikin Films, 2010. DVD.

Blue Gold. Directed by Sam Bozzo. Irvine, CA: Purple Turtle Films, 2010. DVD.

Carbon Nation. Directed by Peter Byck. Louisville, KY: Earth School Educational Foundation, 2010. DVD.

Climate Refugees. Directed by Michael P. Nash. Beverly Hills, CA: L.A. Think Tank, 2010. DVD.

Cool It. Directed by Ondi Timoner. Hollywood, CA: 1019 Entertainment, 2010. DVD.

Erin Brockovich. Directed by Steven Soderbergh. Los Angeles: Jersey Films, 2000. DVD.

The Fifth Estate, "The Denial Machine," CBC, January 7, 2007. Written by Bob McKeown. Directed by Morris Karp. http://www.cbc.ca/fifth/denialmachine/video.html.

Flow: For Love of Water. Directed by Irena Salina. New York: Group Entertainment, 2008. DVD.

Food, Inc. Directed by Robert Kenner. New York: Magnolia Pictures, 2010. DVD.

Frontline, "Climate of Doubt," PBS, October 23, 2012. Written by John Hockenberry and Catherine Upin. Directed by Catherine Upin. http://www.pbs.org/wgbh/pages/frontline/climate-of-doubt/.

GasLand. Directed by Josh Fox. New York: HBO Documentary Films, 2010. DVD.

Greedy Lying Bastards. Directed by Craig Scott Rosebraugh. Los Angeles: 1 Earth Productions, 2013. DVD.

An Inconvenient Truth. Directed by Davis Guggenheim. Los Angeles: Lawrence Bender Productions, 2006. DVD.

Last Call at the Oasis. Directed by Jessica Yu. Los Angeles: Participant Media, 2012. DVD.

Moyers & Company, "The United States of ALEC," PBS, September 30, 2012. Written by Bill Moyers. http://billmoyers.com/episode/full-show-united-states-of-alec/.

National Geographic: Human Footprint. Directed by Clive Maltby. Surrey, UK: Touch Productions, 2008. DVD.

Pricele$$. Directed by Steve Cowan. Portland, OR: Habitat Media, 2010. http://www.pricelessmovie.org.

A River of Waste. Directed by Don McCorkell. Los Angeles: Cinema Libre Studio, 2009. DVD.

Trade Secrets. Written by Bill Moyers and Sherry Jones. New York: Moyers & Company, 2001. http://billmoyers.com/content/trade-secrets/.

Vanishing of the Bees. Directed by George Langworthy and Maryam Henein. Los Angeles: Hive Mentality, 2011. DVD.

Wal-Mart: The High Cost of Low Price. Directed by Robert Greenwald. Culver City, CA: Brave New Films, 2005. DVD.

Waste = Food. Directed by Rob van Hattum. http://topdocumentaryfilms.com/waste-food/.

What Would Jesus Buy? Directed by Rob VanAlkemade. New York: Palisades Pictures, 2007. DVD.

Suggested Resources

Complete bibliographical information on sources not given here can be found in the Bibliography, beginning on page 176.

CHECKING THE FACTS

Snopes (website) devotes scholarly diligence to rumors, photos-gone-viral, and other statements that often pass for fact in popular culture. More people are alive now than all those who've died? Find out. www.snopes.com.

FactCheck (website) applies the Snopes model strictly to politics. www.factcheck.org. The website **PolitiFact** (www.politifact.com) does the same.

FlackCheck (website) describes common rhetorical tricks and posts videos of politicians and media personalities using them to make their positions look better and their opponents look worse. http://www.flackcheck.org/patterns-of-deception.

CLIMATE

Climate Cover-Up: The Crusade to Deny Global Warming **(book)** by James Hoggan, a former PR man himself, ably describes the many facets of the denial campaign.

Deep Future: The Next 100,000 Years of Life on Earth **(book)** by Curt Stager. A paleoecologist peers into the past to get a glimpse of the warmer future. Is Greenland about to melt? Will humans vanish? Balanced, thorough, and a corrective to flimsy "I heard it on TV" opinions. A rare long-distance view and model of the rigorous quest for knowledge.

"Global Warming's Terrifying New Math" (article) by Bill McKibben looks at the consequences and urges us to keep our fossil fuels safely buried. Online at http://www.rollingstone.com/politics/news/global-warmings-terrifying-new-math-20120719.

An Inconvenient Truth **(documentary)** lays out Al Gore's case for global warming and greenhouse gases as the chief cause. His book *Our Choice* examines solutions.

NASA (website). The climate page on NASA's website offers information, maps, images, and interactives about climate. http://climate.nasa.gov.

A Short History of Planet Earth: Mountains, Mammals, Fire, and Ice **(book)** by J. D. MacDougall describes how the climate and creatures we take for granted came to be. The biggest of big pictures, highly recommended.

Skeptical Science (website) gathers the arguments used against the notion that humans are behind global warming and puts them under the microscope. www.skepticalscience.com.

This American Life **(radio show)** offers podcasts of its weekly wide-ranging show at thisamericanlife.org. Two of special interest:

> "Hot in My Backyard" (#495, 5-11-13) examines possible cracks in the climate stalemate in the United States.

> "Game Changer" (#440, 7-8-11) looks at how Pennsylvania is dealing with its huge new finds of natural gas.

The Worst Hard Time: The Untold Story of Those Who Survived the Great American Dust Bowl **(book)** by Timothy Egan (Boston: Houghton Mifflin, 2006). A powerful account of America's first climate refugees.

DATA

Population Clock (website) gives real-time estimates of U.S. and world population, with further information on age, gender, region, and density. http://www.census.gov/popclock.

Worldometers (website) gives population data as well as figures on spending, health, food, energy, and environment. www.worldometers.info.

CO2Now. org (website) gives the latest CO_2 level in the atmosphere. http://co2now.org.

EDUCATION AND INSPIRATION

The Big Here Quiz (website). Learning the facts of life is crucial. This thirty-four-question quiz by *Wired* editor Kevin Kelly is a great place to start, revealing how little most of us know about the place we live in. Prizes offered for high scores; new questions solicited. http://kk.org/cooltools/archives/957.

***Bury the Chains: Prophets and Rebels in the Fight to Free an Empire's Slaves* (book)** by Adam Hochschild (Boston: Houghton Mifflin, 2005). Twelve men meet in a London printshop in 1787, determined to end the British slave trade. They succeed, beating huge vested interests and inventing many of the political tools in use today. The book to read when you think the odds are impossible.

TED (website) offers videos of presentations, all under twenty minutes, at its worldwide conferences devoted to innovative thinking. The TEDxYouth channel on YouTube has talks by high school students. www.ted.com.

Zooniverse (website) applies crowdsourcing to science, using volunteers in all manner of citizen-science projects, from searching for new planets to working on cancer cures, with nothing more than a computer required. www.zooniverse.org.

ENVIRONMENTAL NEWS

(websites)

Climate Desk (www.climatedesk.org)

EnviroClub (www.enviroclub.org)

Environmental News Network (www.enn.com)

Grist (www.grist.org)

Inside Climate News (www.insideclimatenews.org)

Worldwatch (www.worldwatch.org)

FOLLOWING THE MONEY

***(Astro)Turf Wars* (documentary)** investigates the spread of fake grassroots groups disguised to speak for business on issues from health care to climate to taxes.

OpenSecrets.org (website). Who are your congressperson's top donors? Where are political donations percolating through your city and state? Open Secrets covers the intersection of money and politics, with info on lobbying, campaign funding, and much more.

Pricele$$ (documentary) portrays money's influence on U.S. politics, with a focus on energy interests. It streams at http://www.pricelessmovie.org.

SourceWatch.org (website). Not sure if you're dealing with a front group? SourceWatch offers detailed information on hundreds of them. www.sourcewatch.org/index.php/Front_groups.

"The United States of ALEC" (TV show episode) by veteran journalist Bill Moyers shows business in the act of writing the laws that regulate it. It streams at http://billmoyers.com/episode/full-show-united-states-of-alec.

FOOD AND WATER

Fast Food Nation: The Dark Side of the All-American Meal (book) by Eric Schlosser. The strange history of McDonald's, the stranger life of a french fry, and why you don't want to work in a slaughterhouse. Investigative journalism at its best. The basis for the young-adult book *Chew on This* by the same author.

Food, Inc. (documentary) looks at industrial agriculture's effect on our health and environment.

Food and Water Watch (website) offers coverage of food and water issues, from farmed fish to desalination. www.foodandwaterwatch.org.

Food Rights Network (website) has the latest news on food safety issues. www.foodrightsnetwork.org.

Last Call at the Oasis (documentary). Examine a glass of tap water and you'll see most of the themes of this book, from side effects to money to government. This film offers a good look at water issues in the United States.

"Power Steer" (article) by Michael Pollan follows one steer from birth to butcher, revealing how much fossil fuel is hidden in industrially produced meat. Online at http://michaelpollan.com/articles-archive/power-steer/.

Saving the Ocean (TV show). Population, pollution, overfishing, and climate have all put the oceans in peril. Carl Safina's show looks at those who are working to protect and restore them. Streams at http://video.pbs.org/program/saving-the-ocean.

Vanishing of the Bees (documentary) examines collapsing bee colonies through the eyes of two Florida beekeepers, then widens its lens to look at the larger issues of monocultures, pesticides, and politics.

POPULATION

The Habitable Planet (website) looks at many sides of population. http://www.learner.org/courses/envsci/.

Population Connection (website) has a great video that lets you watch world population grow over the past two thousand years. www.populationconnection.org.

"Beyond 7 Billion" (article) is the *Los Angeles Times'* first-rate, five-part report on population. Online, with photos and videos, at http://www.latimes.com/news/nationworld/world/population.

PROBLEM SOLVERS

***Blessed Unrest: How the Largest Movement in the World Came into Being and Why No One Saw It Coming* (book)** by Paul Hawken. Are the thousands of groups working on environmental and social problems part of a super-organism? A jaw-dropping catalog, connected to the website wiser.org.

The Long Now Foundation (website) cultivates long-term thinking through streaming lectures and projects as diverse as competitive predicting and the building of a ten-thousand–year clock. www.longnow.org.

"The Power of Crowds" (radio show episode) on the TED Radio Hour features innovative use of crowds and computers to share news, build hardware, make music, and create surprise. http://www.npr.org/programs/ted-radio-hour.

Transition United States (website) is the U.S. hub for the international transition movement promoting lower energy and more self-sufficient communities. www.transitionus.org.

***Waste = Food* (documentary)** profiles William McDonough and Michael Braungart, the American architect and German chemist who founded the cradle-to-cradle movement. Streams at http://topdocumentaryfilms.com/waste-food. Also see their books *Cradle to Cradle: Remaking the Way We Make Things* and *The Upcycle: Beyond Sustainability — Designing for Abundance*.

WHAT TO BUY

Climate Counts (website) rates companies by their carbon footprints and public support for or against climate legislation. If you're trying to decide between an HP printer and a Canon, this site is for you. www.climatecounts.org.

Cradle to Cradle (website) certifies products that have been designed to exclude pollution problems throughout their life cycles. www.c2ccertified.org.

Environmental Working Group (website) offers safety ratings of personal-care products at its Skin Deep Cosmetics Database. http://www.ewg.org/skindeep.

GoodGuide (website) rates more than 100,000 products by their record on health, environment, and social responsibility. Offers a toolbar that instantly rates products when you're shopping online, as well as a phone app that lets you get info by scanning a product's barcode. www.goodguide.com.

The Good Stuff Guide (website) offers environmental information on common purchases, from computers to chocolate. http://www.worldwatch.org/bookstore/publication /good-stuff-behind-scenes-guide-things-we-buy.

***Overdressed: The Shockingly High Cost of Cheap Fashion* (book)** by Elizabeth L. Cline. The clothes in your closet come from many hidden worlds. This book gives you a tour.

The Story of Stuff (website) has animated films and print information on electronics, bottled water, cosmetics, and consumption's connection to politics. www.storyofstuff.com.

***Wal-Mart: The High Cost of Low Price* (documentary)** looks at the side effects of the low prices we love.

Glossary

ADAPTATION: Doing what we can to counter the effects of climate change: building seawalls, upgrading storm water systems, developing drought-tolerant crops.

ANTHROPOGENIC: Caused by humans.

ANTI-INTELLECTUALISM: The tendency to trust common sense more than the claims of the well educated.

AQUIFER: An underground supply of fresh water, accessed by pumping.

ASTROTURF GROUP: A fake grassroots group, designed to appear to be an association of common citizens but actually orchestrated by business interests to be a mouthpiece for their views.

BIOFUEL: Fuels we manufacture from biological materials, such as ethanol made from corn, biogas from the breakdown of manure or landfill waste, and biomass (see below).

BIOMASS: Usually refers to wood chips burned to produce electricity, often in power plants originally designed to burn coal.

BOTTOM LINE: The profit or loss produced by a business or product.

BRIDGE FUEL: A relatively safe fuel we can burn while we put a green energy system in place. Often used to describe natural gas.

CAP AND TRADE: An attempt to limit pollutants by assigning large emitters a cap and requiring them to buy permits from less-polluting companies to emit more than their cap allows. Also known as *emissions trading.*

CARBON CAPTURE AND STORAGE (CCS): A process to reduce greenhouse gases by liquefying and burying the CO_2 produced by power plants burning fossil fuels.

CARBON DIOXIDE: The most important of the greenhouse gases, produced whenever we burn wood, coal, oil, or natural gas.

CARBON NEUTRAL: Having all the greenhouse gases produced by an activity balanced by an equal amount prevented or sequestered.

CARBON OFFSETS: Donations to programs trying to reduce greenhouse gases through tree-planting, green-energy research, promoting mass transit, and other means. Also called *carbon credits.*

CARBON TAX: Like cap and trade, an attempt to give greenhouse-gas producers a financial interest in emitting less, usually by adding a tax to fossil fuels burned by power plants, industries, or cars.

CARRYING CAPACITY: An area's ability to support population.

CFCs (chlorofluorocarbons): Compounds commonly used in refrigerators, air-conditioners, aerosols, and cleaning solvents. Discovered in the 1980s to be breaking down ozone in the atmosphere.

CHINDIA: A term for the combination of China and India.

Glossary

CLIMATEGATE: The 2009 uproar over hacked e-mails from climatologists that were claimed to prove scientists had manipulated data to support their global-warming views.

COGNITIVE DISSONANCE: The mental tension created by holding two conflicting opinions.

CONFIRMATION BIAS: The tendency to seek out and agree with information that supports our beliefs, leading us to avoid what doesn't.

CONVENTIONALLY GROWN: Grown using synthetic fertilizers and pesticides.

CORNUCOPIANS: Those who dispute claims of scarcity, believing human ingenuity will always keep supplies of food and resources ahead of demand.

CREEPING NORMALCY: The phenomenon that can cause us not to notice big changes that occur gradually over long periods.

CROWDSOURCING: Drawing on the public (especially those online) for ideas, information, and help.

DECENTRALIZATION: Redistributing population from urban to rural areas; taking powers that are concentrated (such as growing food and producing energy) and spreading them widely.

DEFENSE MECHANISMS: Mental maneuvers that ward off doubt, fear, and other uncomfortable feelings.

DEMOGRAPHERS: Scientists who study population.

DENIAL: A defense mechanism that rejects unwelcome information.

DEVELOPING COUNTRIES: Predominantly rural nations. Also called the *Third World*. India, China, and other rapidly industrializing countries are usually included in this category.

DIVEST: To remove one's financial investment.

DOWNCYCLING: Converting waste into materials of lesser quality.

ECOSYSTEM SERVICES: Free but extremely valuable services provided by plants, insects, and other parts of the environment, from pollinating our crops to fighting erosion to protecting coastlines during hurricanes.

EMBARGO: An intentional breakdown in trade.

ENERGY PORTFOLIO: The mix of energy sources drawn upon to produce electricity. Renewable portfolio standards, requiring increasing use of renewables, are becoming common in the United States.

ENVIRONMENTAL JUSTICE: The notion that exposure to pollution shouldn't fall disproportionately on the poor.

EXTERNALIZE: To shift costs outside of a business.

FALLACY: Misguided thinking or a verbal trick used to deceive and sway.

FOSSIL FUELS: Coal, oil, and natural gas, all formed in the Earth from ancient plant or animal remains, and the fuels derived from them, from gasoline to heating oil.

FRACKING: The pumping of water and chemicals into rock formations at high pressure to force out oil and natural gas. Also called *hydraulic fracturing*.

FREE MARKET: An economy in which our transactions — how much we're willing to pay and to whom — set prices and regulate companies' behavior, without government intervening.

FRONT GROUP: A group whose name is meant to hide who's funding it and what it's promoting.

GEOENGINEERING: Large-scale human intervention in the Earth's atmosphere, oceans, and other systems in pursuit of slowing global warming.

GEOTHERMAL POWER: Energy coming from the Earth's own heat, used to heat water and make electricity.

GMOs: Genetically modified organisms with handpicked genes chosen for increased yield, drought endurance, and other attributes. Also known as *GE (genetically engineered) foods.*

GRASSROOTS: Growing spontaneously out of citizens' attitudes.

GREEN REVOLUTION: The technological leaps — especially in plant breeding, pesticides, and herbicides — that dramatically increased food production in the second half of the twentieth century.

GREENHOUSE GASES: Gases such as carbon dioxide, methane, water vapor, and ozone that trap the heat radiating from the Earth.

GREENWASHING: A company's attempt to look more environmentally friendly than it is.

GRID: The network that distributes electricity.

HYDROELECTRIC POWER: Electricity produced by turbines turned by falling water. Also called *hydropower.*

HYPOCRISY: Inconsistent beliefs and deeds, especially the promotion of a public image that's at odds with less public actions.

INFRASTRUCTURE: The basic ingredients needed by communities and businesses, from roads to power stations to lighting.

JUNK SCIENCE: The pursuit of desired conclusions, avoiding rigorous methods and unchecked by peer review.

LAUNDERING: The attempt to hide the source of something. Lobbies launder influence by making anonymous donations or channeling money through foundations that don't reveal their funding sources.

LIFE-CYCLE ANALYSIS (LCA): Looking at all of a product's ingredients and processes from manufacture through disposal.

LOBBYING: The attempt to influence politicians, usually through persuasion and campaign donations. A lobby is a group with a common agenda.

METHANE: A greenhouse gas, shorter lived than CO_2 but much more effective at trapping heat.

MITIGATION: The effort to reduce the causes of climate change, especially cutting greenhouse gases and slowing deforestation.

Glossary

MONOCULTURE: Raising large numbers of the same plant or animal in one place.

MUCKRAKING: Journalism that digs up unpleasant truths, usually about powerful institutions.

NEWLY INDUSTRIALIZED COUNTRIES (NICs): Countries well on the way toward Western economies and living standards. Examples: China, India, Brazil, Indonesia, Mexico, South Africa, Thailand, Turkey, Malaysia, the Philippines.

NORMALCY BIAS: Reluctance to take seriously a disaster that's never happened to us before.

PEAK OIL: The moment when the amount of oil we can pump begins declining due to limited supply.

PEER REVIEW: The checking of a scientific paper for accuracy by other scientists considered experts on the subject.

POSITIVE FEEDBACK LOOP: A process in which effects magnify the causes that are producing the effects, leading to upward-spiraling outcomes.

PRODUCER RESPONSIBILITY LAWS: Requirements that manufacturers must pay for the collection and recycling of their discarded products. Also called *Extended Producer Responsibility (EPR) laws.*

PROJECTION: A defense mechanism that deflects blame by claiming that the accuser is guilty of the charge.

PUBLIC RELATIONS (PR): The attempt to influence the public's attitudes toward products, politicians, and policies, most often through messages planted in the media.

RACE TO THE BOTTOM: The quest to get products' prices as low as possible, achieved through paying rock-bottom wages, neglecting worker and product safety, and avoiding environmental responsibility.

RARE EARTH ELEMENTS: Important ingredients in cell phones, lasers, batteries, and lighting. They're not rare but are usually dispersed rather than concentrated.

RATIONALIZATION: Concocting reasons to justify our actions, a defense mechanism we use when we're troubled by our deeds or beliefs.

REGRESSION: The defense mechanism that rescues us from worry by encouraging a retreat to childlike irresponsibility.

RESOURCE CURSE: The downsides that can befall a country after it discovers a valuable resource such as oil or diamonds.

SHALE: Rock that was once mud. Recent large finds of shale oil and shale gas have been made in the United States.

SHIFTING BASELINES: The phenomenon in which our judgments are thrown off by a baseline limited to our own lifetime. This can lead to each generation seeing a steadily degrading environment as normal.

SINKS: The oceans, air, soil, and plants that store pollutants.

SLASH-AND-BURN: A method of agriculture in which farmers clear forest, plant crops, and move on a few years later when the soil has lost its fertility.

SMALL GOVERNMENT: Government that keeps taxes and regulation of business to a minimum.

SOVEREIGN: Independent of outside control.

SUBSIDIES: Government payments to businesses to promote the production of desired goods.

SUPPLY CHAIN: The web of companies supplying the various materials that business needs.

TAX BREAKS: Tax reductions that government bestows to support businesses it feels are vital.

THINK TANKS: Institutions that produce research on particular topics from a particular slant, usually with the aim of influencing public opinion and policies.

THIRD PARTY: A website or company that rates other companies' products for safety, environmental impact, labor practices, and similar factors. Because those who rate aren't the ones making the product, a vested-interests conflict is avoided, giving third-party certifications more weight.

THIRD WORLD: See DEVELOPING COUNTRIES.

THRESHOLD: An invisible border beyond which noticeable effects are produced.

TRADE GROUP: A lobbying group that represents an industry as a whole.

TRAGEDY OF THE COMMONS: The pressure to overexploit a shared resource, like fish or grazing land, until it's destroyed.

TRANSPARENCY: Full disclosure of a business's supply chain, manufacturing practices, treatment of employees, and environmental impact.

UNCONVENTIONAL ENERGY: Energy sources that require much extra money, equipment, and processes to extract and refine, such as deep-sea oil, tar sands, and shale gas.

UPCYCLING: Using recycled goods to make products of higher rather than lower quality.

VESTED INTEREST: Loyalty to a business, policy, philosophy, etc. that is driven by financial or emotional investment.

THE WEST: The most affluent nations, including the United States, Canada, Japan, Australia, and the countries of western Europe.

Acknowledgments

What began as a slim, simple book evolved over the years into a more complex creature. Along the way, I incurred many debts. I'm happy to have the chance to thank:

Flannery Fitch for much help with clippings and the bibliography.

Mica Quintana for her labors in the labyrinths of newspaper databases.

Noël Chilton for her ideas on design.

Milton Love and Rowan Jacobsen for their expert testimony.

Debbie Van Dyke and Peter Cardellichio for their writer's-dream retreat.

Ethan Bronstein, Spencer Merritt, Julie Wiley, Scott Zgraggen, and Ryan Alpers for field-testing the book.

Elin Kelsey for much thoughtful critiquing.

Joyce Valenza, Shannon Miller, and Ross McClenahan for taking the book into the digital realm.

Marc Aronson, John Glenn, Georgia Rucker, and Sarah Parvis for the enthusiasm, wisdom, care, and flair they bestowed on the book's look and content. This was literary chamber music at its best.

Liz Bicknell, Kaylan Adair, Jon Bresman, and the team at Candlewick Press for making that vision flesh.

And my wife, Patty Brown, for all of the above and more.

Image Credits

Index

Italic page numbers indicate illustrations or photographs.

Page numbers ending in *n* indicate information found in the Source Notes.

Index

Index

Index

Index

Index

A Book by Aronson & Glenn LLC
Produced by Marc Aronson & John W. Glenn
Cover and interior design by Georgia Rucker

First edition 2014

Library of Congress Catalog Card Number 2013953458
ISBN 978-0-7636-7102-0 (hardcover)
ISBN 978-0-7636-7545-5 (paperback)

14 15 16 17 18 19 SHD 10 9 8 7 6 5 4 3 2 1

Printed in Ann Arbor, MI, U.S.A.

This book was typeset in Avenir, Chaparral, ITC American Typewriter,
ITC Highlander, and URW Egyptienne.

Candlewick Press
99 Dover Street
Somerville, Massachusetts 02144

visit us at www.candlewick.com